The Cassock and the Crown
Canada's Most Controversial Murder Trial

The prosecution of a Roman Catholic priest for the murder of his brother, l'affaire Delorme captured the public imagination not only in Canada but throughout the world. On 7 January 1922 Raoul Delorme's body was discovered in a Montreal suburb. He had been shot six times at close range. The victim's half-brother, Father Adélard Delorme, quickly became the prime suspect. Circumstantial evidence point directly to him: police, in one of the first uses of ballistics, matched the bullets used in the murder to a gun he had purchased only days before the murder, there were human bloodstains in his car, and the victim's body was wrapped in a quilt that matched others found at the Delorme house. He had also recently taken out a life insurance policy on his brother, naming himself as beneficiary, and stood to inherit most of the family's estate under Raoul's will.

The Roman Catholic church, however, was an extremely powerful institution in Quebec in the 1920s. Four trials took place before a verdict was reached – a verdict that still leaves many questions unanswered.

A fascinating true story, *The Cassock and the Crown* is based on trial transcripts, interviews with individuals involved in the case, and twenty-five years of archival research. It provides insight into Quebec culture in the 1920s and is a topical look, in light of recent celebrity trials, at the subjective nature of the judicial system when it deals with people in positions of prestige and power.

JEAN MONET, QC, is the grandson of Dominique Monet, the presiding judge at one of the trials. He has been practising law in Montreal since 1957.

THE
CASSOCK
AND THE
CROWN

CANADA'S
MOST CONTROVERSIAL
MURDER TRIAL

Jean Monet

McGill-Queen's University Press
Montreal & Kingston • London • Buffalo

© McGill-Queen's University Press 1996
ISBN 0-7735-1399-X (cloth)
ISBN 0-7735-1449-X (paper)

Legal deposit first quarter 1996
Bibliothèque nationale du Québec

Printed in Canada on acid-free paper

McGill-Queen's University Press is grateful
to the Canada Council
for support of its publishing program.

Canadian Cataloguing in Publication Data

Monet, Jean, 1932–
The cassock and the crown
ISBN 0-7735-1399-X (bound) –
ISBN 0-7735-1449-X (pbk.)
1. Delorme, Adélard. 2. Murderers – Quebec
(Province) – Montréal. 3. Murder – Quebec
(Province) – Montréal – Investigation.
4. Trials (Murder) – Quebec (Province) –
Montréal. 5. Priests – Quebec (Province) –
Biography. I. Title.
HV6248.D45M6613 1996   C95-920877-1
364.1'523'0971428

Typeset in Janson Text 10/12
by Caractéra inc., Quebec City

*To Barbara, Peter, Marcie, Dallas,
and to the memory of Fabio.*

Contents

Preface   ix

Foreword: Locus in Quo by Jacques Monet   xiii

Illustrations   xviii

1   December 1921: Home for Christmas   3

2   Epiphany 1922: A Body on Ice   6

3   The Investigation   7

4   A Question of Sanity   51

5   The Evidence   85

6   The Art of Persuasion   117

7   Deja Vu   133

8   The Verdict   146

9   Who Killed Raoul?   151

Epilogue   157

Preface

This book has been an on-again off-again hobby of mine for about twenty-five years. I think I was meant to write it: it's a real-life murder mystery, has an important connection to my family, and took place in Montreal, the city I was brought up in, live in, work in, and love. During my research, I couldn't help but be sidetracked time and again by interesting anecdotes about its history and citizens.

The story began with the discovery of a young man's body on 7 January 1922 in the Snowdon area of Montreal. The controversial police investigation which followed led to the victim's brother, a priest, being accused of his murder.

L'affaire Delorme soon took on international notoriety, not only because Montreal's social fabric was strongly influenced by the Roman Catholic Church but also because of the personality of the accused and the lifestyle of his family. Four trials were required before the final outcome. The press quickly labelled the first "the trial of the century." The trials involved a renowned detective, a bevy of psychiatric experts, some of the greatest legal talent in Canada, and the expertise of Dr Wilfrid Derome, father of forensic medicine on this continent. The Delorme trial introduced the use of ballistics in criminal cases in North America and was one of the first to involve blood type comparisons and other forensic techniques. The case shook the city to its very foundation. Its final result left Montrealers with many unanswered questions, not only about the crime and the trials but about themselves.

As a youngster, I had sometimes heard my father talk about L'affaire Delorme and I vaguely understood that it was connected with my grandfather's death. A judge, he had presided at the first trial. But I never really paid much attention to what was being said – I was more interested in getting on with my own activities.

In the fall of 1957, my father died. In the weeks that followed, as I was cleaning out his files I came across a couple of boxes full of documents, letters, depositions, newspaper reports, and pieces of evidence concerning Delorme. They were my late grandfather's files. I was fascinated by what I saw and thought that writing a book about L'affaire Delorme might not only be fun as a hobby but could uncover an important story that had been kept under wraps since the mid 1920s. But it would have to wait; I had just started my career as a practising lawyer and there were other priorities.

In early 1969 I met with Gustave Monette, the first of Delorme's many lawyers. Then eighty-two years of age, Mr Monette told me everything he remembered about the case and was kind enough to make his files available to me. A dozen or so years later I set up a loosely organized research schedule and over the next few years I spent many hours gathering information in the archives of various newspapers, le ministère de la Justice, and other judicial and religious institutions. I also interviewed people directly or indirectly involved in the case. In this phase of my project Gérard Monette (no relation to Gustave) from Le Centre de documentation of La Presse was of great assistance in helping me find newspaper reports and photographs of the case. Arthur Perrault, librarian of The Montreal Bar, Maurice de Gagné, Dr André Lauzon, director of forensic medicine of the Montreal Crime Laboratory, Gaétan Levreault and André Munch, technicians at the crime lab, Monique Montbriand, archivist at The Montreal Chancery Office, and Erménégilde Laflamme, archivist at The Institute for the Deaf and Dumb were also most generous in providing me with their time and relevant data. Rosario Farah-Lajoie and his sisters Laurence Lamoureux and Ghislaine Farah-Lajoie Robin gave me fascinating information about their father Georges Farah-Lajoie's involvement in the case and how it affected their family life. Isi Cohen, Guy Poliquin, and Brian Aboud gave me interesting information for the epilogue while Ivoj Kudrnac opened my eyes to the versatility of ether. The Honourable Fred Kaufman, formerly of the Court of Appeal, helped clarify questions about court proceedings in criminal trials. During the fine-tuning of my manuscript, Marisa Iasenza and Nishi Aubin were of great help digging out various articles and reports from libraries and newspaper archives. My beautiful teenage daughter, Marcie, interrupted her all-important driving lessons to rush around libraries for last-minute research on Bayard pistols and Franklin cars.

By the late 1980s I had accumulated enough material to write my first manuscript. First, I had to decide whether to present the information as a novel based on my research but interwoven with fictional content or an account of what happened. I decided on the latter. The only places where the reader will find literary licence are the first and last chapters. Otherwise, my book is faithful to Georges Farah-Lajoie's report of the police investigation and to the testimony given at the coroner's inquest, the preliminary hearing, and each of the subsequent four trials as recorded in the official transcripts of those hearings. I also took material from the many newspaper accounts published in Canada, the United States, and abroad. When referring to or quoting a newspaper report or editorial I have always attempted to give the name and date. Where such is omitted, there is a good reason – the only copy I could find didn't have that information. An example of this is an unnamed publication I quote in the context of public reaction after the first trial. I found the quoted article in my grandfather's files. It had been so neatly cut out from the publication that nothing was left but the text itself.

I hope the reader will forgive me for having given my grandfather Dominique more than equal time. Born on 2 January 1865 in the small farming village of Napierville on the outskirts of Montreal, he was a farmer's son who was chosen for a college education and went on to inspire generations of Monets and Monettes* to become lawyers and judges. In many ways, this book is for him.

I wrote two manuscripts, one in French, the other in English, and completed them at about the same time. Being a Montreal story, I decided to publish the French version first.† It was launched in May of 1993 and generated additional information from readers who were familiar with some aspects of the case.

Quite a few people read my manuscript at various stages of its development. Joanne Bauer, Richard Bauer, Julia Corbin, Harry Gulkin, Ethel Hanel, Ginette Gaulin Lachance, Eugene La Comte, Gilles Lauzon, Bob Leisenring, my late cousin the Honourable Amedée Monet and my former partner the Honourable Gerald McCarthy, both judges of the Court of Appeal, Frank Reedy, my son Peter, who as a teenager became a literary critic at the mandatory rate of twenty pages a day, Dallas's godmother Michèle Tanguay, and Doris Tooby. Collectively, they gave me a great deal of encouragement and many helpful ideas.

---

* The family name is recorded as Monette in Dominique's birth certificate but Monet in his death certificate. Dominique shortened it when he discovered that the family name in France had been Monet and that the last syllable had been added in Canada to reflect the French Canadian pronunciation.

† *La Soutane et la Couronne* (Montréal: Les Éditions du Trécarré, 1993).

My brother Jacques, one of Canada's leading historians, not only reviewed my original manuscript but took time out of his busy schedule to write the Foreword, giving the reader an overview of the cultural background of Montreal against which this drama was played.

When I thought it was time, I sent my manuscript to Philip Cercone, Executive Director of McGill-Queen's University Press. I was delighted to receive his positive reply. We discussed it over a couple of lunches (the second on him) and he then turned me over to the budget-conscious but otherwise delightful combo of Joan McGilvray, Coordinating Editor, and Susanne McAdam, Production and Design Manager. Despite the fact that neither of them realized my manuscript was the only thing of any importance in the whole wide world, they were a pleasure to work with and did a highly professional job. Finally, a book emerged.

I owe much to my secretaries Ginette Ouellet, Marie-Andrée Laperrière, Marie-France Lamoureux, and Lynda Boissonneault. Each of them worked far beyond the call of duty. Giles Rivest was very accommodating in preparing photographs of the trial exhibits.

That is almost the complete story of how *The Cassock and the Crown* came to be. "Almost" because I have not yet mentioned my lovely wife, Barbara, who not only helped me with both the research and the manuscript but was invaluable in providing me with ideas, support, and encouragement throughout all this.

It was a time-consuming but wondrous experience. *Merci beaucoup* to all of the people mentioned above. Now that it's done, I'm going to take up golf.

Jean Monet
Montreal
28 December 1995

Locus in Quo

It does seem strange that a murder mystery that so captured the public imagination in its own time – a story so crowded with eccentric characters and odd behaviour, so thick with complicated plots, curious coincidences, and unexpected turns, so rich in courtroom drama, sinister undertones, and violence bred on bigotry and greed – should have gone unexamined for so long. One would think that by now *l'affaire Delorme* would have become a solid part of the anthologies of the western world's great unsolved criminal investigations. Instead, it remains almost unknown. This is unfortunate, for the case offers an intriguing look at a particular place and time.

For a historian, the early 1920s in French Canada are a very fertile area. Things were looking up. The trauma caused by crises over French schools in Ontario and conscription was healing. A new administration in Ottawa had been elected with overwhelming Québécois support, leading to the feeling that the government of Canada was once more being conducted, and its principal policies formulated, with proper attention paid to Quebec. In Quebec, a new administration was committed to continuing the kind of policies that, by attracting American investment, especially in the pulp and paper industries, would secure both the economic prosperity and the social stability that the province needed ... and wanted.

Montreal, the second largest French-speaking city in the world, was prosperous and powerful. It was the Dominion's main seat of commerce and industry as well as its most populated urban centre (714,000 people in 1921), a city of great charm, variety, and vivacity, it was said by European travellers to be one of the most appealing cities in North America and certainly French Canadians, then almost 60 per cent of its population, took great and increasing pride in it.

By the mid-1920s its leaders in business (often Protestant and English) and politics (mostly Catholic and French) could boast of completing a new plan for improving the harbour that would make Montreal the greatest grain export centre in the world and, after New York, the largest port in North America. They could also point to the engineering feat of a railway tunnel under Mount Royal that contributed greatly to the movement of both people and industrial goods (there were some 2,800 factories in Montreal in the early 1920s) to and from the new and spreading suburbs; or to the up-to-date snow-removal equipment, required for the wider streets needed to accommodate increasing numbers of new automobiles, buses, and trucks; or to the opening of modern headquarters for the Bank of Montreal, the Royal Bank of Canada, and the Canadian National Railway, all established in 1924 after a succession of intricate and, for Montrealers, profitable mergers. The opening of a new school of Fine Arts and two very rewarding fundraising campaigns ($3,000,000 and $5,000,000 respectively) for McGill University and the Université de Montréal securely established Montreal as an important cultural capital as well.

By the early 1920s French Canadians had become an urban and industrialized people. During the last generation they had left the land for the city in the tens of thousands, and had moved – mostly – into the central east end of Montreal. There, on new streets in row on row of new houses with spiralling corkscrew staircases, they signalled their growing share in the city's overall prosperity. Whatever their previous relation to the stereotype of Quebec as a settled, static society of *habitant* farmers and lumberjacks, cut off from "progress" by distinctive laws, language, and Catholic religion, inhabited by unambitious, illiterate, and docile people, ploughing fields in the shadow of the village church, it was certainly no longer relevant.

At the recently created Université de Montréal, however, an intense and self-centred group of *nationalistes* disciples, led by a young professor of history, Abbé Lionel Groulx, were being indoctrinated by an ideal which they were, I think, already far too well-disposed to follow. This was that the survival of their nationality depended not on the kind of urban development going on in Montreal but on conserving precisely the traditional values of the agricultural society of the *ancien régime* they had just abandoned. Groulx considered these values, the French language, and the clerical institutions of the Catholic Church to be the essential ingredients of the Quebec nationality. Another compelling exaltation of the traditional values of land, language, and religion was found in Louis Hémon's recent and best-selling novel *Maria Chapdelaine*. Towards the end of that peasant idyll, (and by the early 1920s, large numbers of French Canadians knew the following passage by heart) the Province of Quebec takes on a human voice, "half a woman's song and half a priest's sermon" to proclaim:

Three hundred years ago, we settled on this land, and everything we brought with us, our religion, our language, our virtues, and even our weaknesses, have now become sacred things. We are surrounded by aliens, who have seized almost all the power and taken almost all the money, but we know that in centuries to come the world will turn to us and say: "These people are of a race that cannot die".

The fact is however, that the everyday life and experience of the *Montréalais* took place in an industrial, plural, and urban environment, an environment that was not being reflected back in the mirror held up to them by their priests and teachers.

The way of life of French Canadians had in fact changed radically. The land had been left behind, the language was changing. Only Catholic institutions remained apparently unaffected, an impressive symbol of continuity in the new city setting. The silver spires of Saint-Jacques and the Immaculée Conception rose tall above the east end's rooftops, as did the statue of Our Lady on Bonsecours Chapel, whose outstretched arms seemed extended to protect the new improvements in the harbour. The gothic outlines of Notre-Dame, the dome of the cathedral, the rising contours of Brother André's oratory, the illuminated cross atop Mount Royal, all were striking features of Montreal's skyline. The dozens of substantial grey-limestone buildings – schools, colleges, orphanages, hospitals, and old people's homes, each with its chapel – made it clearly evident that the Church continued to dominate. Montreal may have been the only city in the world where, as Mark Twain had said, "You couldn't throw a brickbat without breaking a church window."

The strength of the institutional Church in Quebec made it unique. Having been there since the very beginning of the country's history, and through so many and such drastic social changes, it had become thoroughly entangled in every other civil, political, economic, and cultural organization. By the early 1920s religious brothers, nuns, and priests were presidents of universities, superiors of colleges, school commissioners, principals of high schools and teacher's colleges, founders of credit and labour unions, directors of social services and sports centres, guidance counsellors, hockey coaches, and professors of geometry, latin, and physics. And they all shared the nineteenth-century Catholic view of society as hierarchical, pious, rigorous, and traditional.

The Church's omnipresence and the powerful conservatism and arrogance of authoritarian clerics left its mark on French Canadians. Many became angry or fearful. Frère Untel, writing his *Insolences* at the end of the 1950s, described a mood which certainly went back to the early 1920s. "We are terribly afraid of authority: we live in a bewitched atmosphere in which we feel that it is a matter of life or death not to infringe any taboo, to respect all the formulae, all the conformities. The diffused fear in which we live sterilizes all our activities." Others, more positive, appreciated the contribution of Roman Catholic organizations. They felt that the Church had pro-tected and guided French Canadians, especially during the decades after the conquest when no other institution could have done so. Most, I think, tended to consider the clergy simply as part of the family. Clerics, they argued, might have been ignorant at times – in some instances absurdly so – but in general they were well-known and well-liked people who fitted easily into society and were easily respected. After all, there were very few French Canadians who did not count a priest as a cousin or nephew, an uncle or a brother.

My brother has asked me to introduce his book. I told him it needed no introduction. He insisted and, frankly, I am honoured, flattered, and delighted. He has taken a long look at what the Delorme case was about. Through exhaustive and factual research in the original records of court, press, and chancery, he has followed many curious trails to arrive at a better understanding of the puzzle. In fascinating detail, he tells what actually happened and suggests what probably happened.

He writes three generations after the events of the case and one after the very gentle revolution (or "the quieter revolution" as I have called it elsewhere) which disentangled the institutions and values of French Canada's church and society. Today, the civil, criminal, and religious aspects of l'affaire Delorme would be dealt with very differ-ently. (In the 1950s a Quebec bishop found guilty of negligence in a car accident was given a suspended sentence; in the 1970s another priest was convicted and jailed for manslaughter). Today, most Québé-cois have left the authoritarian and autocratic Church of the 1920s. Many have truly deepened their understanding of the church's mes-sage. They have a different awareness of the meaning of priestly service. Still, at the level of personal reactions the same kind of   ·

ambiguity and ambivalence may well remain as at the time of our grandparents. Even today, in a case like Delorme's, the accused would, willy-nilly, represent an institution at once fearful and lovable, mysterious and familiar, transcendant and worldly, human and ... divine.

Jacques Monet, sj
The University of Sudbury
29 August 1995

Reverend Adélard Delorme.

Detective Georges Farah-Lajoie.
(Courtesy Laurence Lamoureux)

Raoul Delorme's University of Ottawa yearbook photograph.
(Courtesy Marcel Hamelin)

Re-enactment of the finding of Raoul's body by a municipal
employee in the early morning of 7 January 1922 at the corner
of Coolbrook and Snowdon streets. In the photo, taken at the actual
site, a newspaper photographer's assistant plays Raoul.
On the right is the shed where Montreal municipal employees
stored their equipment.

Rosa Delorme, Adélard Delorme's sister.

Adélard Delorme arriving at the courthouse from Bordeaux Prison.

The Honourable Dominique Monet,
who presided over the first trial in 1922.

The Honourable Sir François Xavier Lemieux, who presided over the second trial in 1923. (Pierre Georges Roy, *Les juges de la province de Québec*, Quebec: le service des archives du gouvernement de la province de Québec, 1933)

Jury for the 1923 trial. First row, left to right, William Hughes, Emeril Duranceau, H.F.B. Powell, Georges Corriveau, G.S. Tiffany, Alfred Plourde. Second row: Alexis Provost, William Niddle, Jules Goyer, Wilfrid David, Daniel Guimond, and P. Décarie.

Adélard Delorme's Iver Johnson and Bayard handguns. Two weeks before the murder Delorme exchanged the larger Iver Johnson for the smaller and quieter Bayard, the alleged murder weapon. He also purchased the two boxes of bullets.

Dr Wilfrid Derome, the forensic expert, built these models for the jury to demonstrate the rotation of a bullet as it travels through the cannon of a revolver and to show the scratches on the bullets found in Raoul's body that matched those on the experimental bullet fired from Delorme's Bayard.

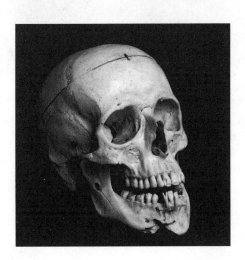

Raoul Delorme's skull. It was passed from juror to juror and carefully examined as Dr Derome explained the path of the bullets. Two of the bullet holes – one in the point of the chin, the other in the side of the jaw – are visible. These items are still in the possession of the Montreal Crime Laboratory. (Photo Giles Rivest)

Adélard Delorme leaving his home after the visit by the court, his first return since having been imprisoned eighteen months earlier. To his far right is Oscar Haynes, the gunsmith from whom he purchased the alleged murder weapon. Next to him is Napoléon Séguin, governor of Bordeaux Prison, with whom Delorme developed a close relationship. Behind him is High Constable Achille Cinq-Mars, a court official.

The crowd assembled at the Delorme residence, alleged site of the murder, before the visit of the court during the 1923 trial. To the left of the front door is the window of Father Delorme's study. The bay window above the front door looks into Raoul's study, where he may have been murdered.

The Honourable Paul Gédéon Martineau, who presided over the third trial in February 1924. (Roy, *Les juges de la province de Québec*)

The Honourable Auguste Maurice Tessier, who presided
over the fourth and last trial in October 1924.
(Roy, *Les juges de la province de Québec*)

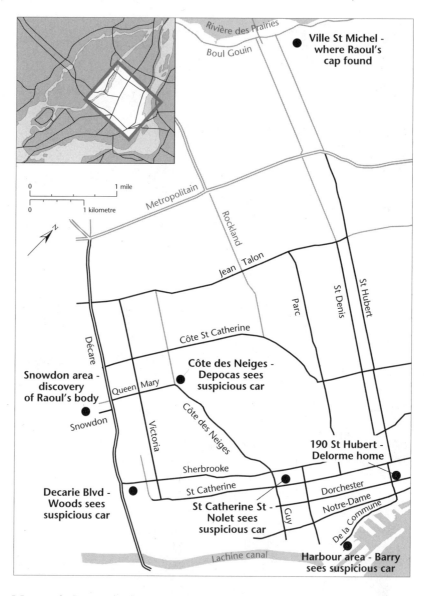

Montreal. Streets built since the time of the Delorme affair are in grey.

The Cassock and the Crown

Home for Christmas

Neither the rhythm of the steel wheels rushing beneath him nor the beauty of the frozen rural scenes flying past his window could disturb Raoul Delorme's thoughts. This was his last Christmas break from the University of Ottawa. After his upcoming graduation he would be finished with school and free to manage his inheritance. He thought about the events of the last few years: his father's death in 1916, his half-brother Adélard's devotion to him and to his sisters and his dedication to managing Raoul's properties. He thought of how Adélard, Monsieur l'Abbé Delorme outside the family home, had obtained a special exemption from parish work from the Roman Catholic Archdiocese of Montreal to allow him to take care of his brother and sisters. The archbishop had even appointed him chaplain of the Public Welfare Service, whose headquarters were a few minutes walk from the rambling Delorme home at 190 St Hubert Street, in the downtown area near the corner of Dorchester Boulevard.* The Delorme family needed Adélard. Two of his three sisters were somewhat slow-witted and unable to handle their own affairs. Raoul himself had been a slow learner and realized that his college degree would be due in large part to Adélard's insistence that he persist in his education. Adélard had even personally arranged to have Raoul accepted at the University of Ottawa. Now, finally, at twenty-four he would end his "cours classique" and receive the much coveted "baccalauréat." With assets of close to $200,000,† a sizeable income,

---

* Now Boulevard René-Lévesque.
† On the basis of a basket of 487 goods and services, in 1994 $8.60 was required to buy what $1.00 would have bought in 1921. Raoul's assets would thus have been about $1,720,000 today (*Statistics Canada Consumer Price Index*, Ottawa: Minister of Supply and Services Canada, 1994).

and a college degree in his hands, he was looking forward to the future.

Raoul felt a touch of sadness at the thought that Adélard would soon have to turn everything over to him, knowing he would miss managing Raoul's properties. Over the years he had grown adept at it and enjoyed negotiating and collecting rentals, arranging for the buildings to be kept in good repair, keeping the books, and doing the banking. "Is it fair" Raoul thought, "to take this away from him?" After all, Adélard was like a combination of father and good friend. He could be severe at times, especially when Raoul asked for money to go to the movies or a restaurant, but, down deep, Raoul knew it was for his own good. And that touch of severity was a small price to pay for the good times he shared with Adélard, especially when the priest treated him by taking him on a long car trip every summer. "At least," Raoul said to himself, "Adélard is so good that he will be happy to see me taking over my own affairs."

His thoughts shifted to his Christmas vacation. He planned to go to a lot of movies and to spend time listening to music on his new gramophone. He was fascinated by the novelty of these instruments and remembered how, a year or so ago, he had marvelled at the regular radio programs started by the Marconi Company. He was old enough now to appreciate Montreal's cosmopolitan flavour and to have shared some of its history, including the effect of the World War. A teenager then, he remembered the conscription riots, the volunteers drilling on the McGill campus, the sobbing women watching their men march through the streets to the waiting trains or to the ships which moved silently down the St Lawrence in the early dawn, taking them to the battlefields of Europe. He also remembered sharing in the celebrations for the returning troops after Armistice Day in 1918. While he had enjoyed his stay in Ottawa, it couldn't compare with Montreal. Despite being the nation's capital, it had a small town mentality, unlike Montreal which, with a population close to one million, was the second largest French-speaking city in the world and a dynamic metropolis. He had become familiar with Ottawa within a few weeks of his arrival, but there were still large areas of Montreal completely unknown to him, despite his having lived in the city for his whole life. For example, he had rarely ventured into the English-speaking section of the city, especially Westmount, considered the bastion of Anglo-Saxon wealth. But living in Ottawa had been a good experience – being away from home had helped turn him into a confident young man.

Familiar landmarks flashed by the window as the train approached downtown Montreal. They reminded Raoul of how terribly impressed he had been with the construction of the Canadian Northern Railway tunnel under Mount Royal in 1918 and the new electric trains that travelled through it.* As a young boy he had often walked all the way to the "canyon" next to Dorchester Boulevard and watched that activity with great interest.† His reminiscing was interrupted by the train conductor's cry, "Next stop, prochain arrêt, Montreal, Windsor station." Raoul couldn't wait to get home.

---

* In early 1911 Sir William McKenzie and Sir Donald Mann, the promoters of the tunnel, acquired property along Dorchester Boulevard and farm land on the north side of Mount Royal. In the fall of that year, authorization was given to build a tunnel under the mountain with a railway station and a hotel at the Dorchester Boulevard end. World War I delayed completion until 1918, but real estate values then skyrocketed at both ends of the tunnel with the development of the downtown Dorchester area and the creation of Model City, later known as the Town of Mount Royal

† A Montreal landmark until the construction of Place Ville Marie in the 1950s, the canyon now lies under the PVM plaza.

EPIPHANY 1922

A Body on Ice

Like almost all French Canadians, on the morning of Friday, 6 January 1922, Euzèbe Larin went to Mass to celebrate Epiphany. "Les Rois," as it was commonly known in Quebec, marked the end of the Christmas religious holidays and their customary family gatherings. The next important date was Easter. Until then there was nothing to look forward to but a long hard winter and the demands of the forty-day fasting period during Lent. It was no wonder that Euzèbe was enthusiastically involved in the Larin family celebration and the traditional selection of the king and queen who would preside over the festivities and their crowning glory, a banquet served by the proud matriarch.

The next day, in the freezing dawn, a rather tired Larin left his home in the Notre Dame de Grâce suburb of Montreal for his job in the Montreal Roads Department. As usual, he passed a toolshed at the corner of Coolbrook and Snowdon avenue. Approaching the shed, he noticed a large dark spot on the frozen ground. A closer look revealed the body of a well-dressed young man, his hands tied and the tails of his overcoat pulled over his head and fastened with safety pins. Larin headed for the closest phone and called the police. A short while later Sergeant Detective Dominique Pusie of the Homicide Department arrived on the scene. Pusie loosened the coat but could see only a frozen, blood-soaked quilt stuck to the victim's face and hair. A quick look around didn't reveal any clues, so he lit a cigarette and waited for the hearse. It arrived a few minutes later and took the body to the Craig Street* morgue.†

---

* Now St Antoine Street.
† In 1922 crime scene protection was not an integral part of police procedure. That didn't happen until the development of forensic medicine, which explains why Pusie didn't have the area cordoned off or conduct an extensive search.

The Investigation

At 11 A.M. on 7 January, Sergeant Detective Théodule Pigeon and Constable Joseph Desgroseillers rang the doorbell at 190 St Hubert Street. To their surprise, a man in a black cassock – Adélard Delorme – came to the door. When asked if this was the residence of Raoul Delorme, he answered nervously, "Yes, Raoul is my brother. Has anything happened to him? Is he in trouble? He didn't come home last night." Pigeon replied that a body carrying Raoul's identity card had been found early that morning and asked the priest to accompany them to the morgue for the necessary identification. "Give me a minute," he replied, "and don't say anything to my sisters." When he saw Raoul's body lying on the morgue floor, Father Delorme stoically muttered "It's him all right," blessed the body with a quick hand motion, and left the room.

A brief coroner's hearing was held on Monday, 9 January, presided over by Coroner Edmond McMahon. His function was to investigate any death not clearly due to natural causes. Only three witnesses appeared before the six-man jury*: Dr Donald MacTaggart, who had helped perform the autopsy, an official from the morgue, and Father Delorme. Dr MacTaggart produced the following report:

Montreal Jan 7th 1922

Autopsy on the body of Raoul Delorme.

Body of a young man of medium build.
Two small wounds on the right side of the face, one near the molar eminence and the other near the chin.

---

* Today no jury is involved in the coroner's inquest.

Six wounds on the anterior surface of the neck. The wrists show depressions caused by a small cord tied around them.

The anterior surface of the right wrist shows broad scratches and there is some discoloration of the back of the hand and some erosions of the skin.

On opening the body two small bullets are found, one in the point of the chin which has fractured the bone and one on the left side of the neck half way between the angle of the jaw and the base of the neck, close to the side of the spine.

The organs of the body were found to be healthy.

CONCLUSIONS Death was caused by bullet wound of the head and neck.

[signed] D. Mac Taggart

Wilfrid Derome

The morgue official produced what he had found on the body: an undated letter from Adélard, a partly torn picture of a young girl, on the reverse side of which appeared the words "Indecent-uncensored," some bogus dollar bills, a Holy Rosary, and the stub of a ticket for the Princess Theatre. He had also removed a quilt from Raoul's head. Father Delorme repeated what he had told the policeman at the morgue: Raoul had gone to a movie the previous afternoon and had telephoned him afterwards to say he had met some friends and wouldn't be sleeping at home. The only new information he provided was that he managed Raoul's assets, which consisted mostly of twenty rental properties that generated an annual income of about $10,000,* and was executor of his father's estate. He himself owned twenty-four rental properties. Coroner McMahon felt there wasn't enough evidence for him to reach a conclusion and adjourned the hearing until the seventeenth. He urged the police to return with more facts.

That day, Police Chief Adrien Lepage called Georges Farah-Lajoie to his office. "I want you to drop everything you're working on, and put all your time and energy toward solving the Delorme murder," Lepage told Farah-Lajoie. A tall, slim, balding man in his mid-forties with piercing eyes and a meticulously honed handlebar mustache, Farah-Lajoie was an internationally renowned detective. Born in Syria, he was a member of the Greek Catholic Church and had studied in Jerusalem to become a priest, planning to work in Africa as a missionary, but had left before taking his final vows. Instead of returning home he travelled to Egypt, Europe, England, and South America, eventually making his way to Montreal in 1900. Two years

---

* The purchasing power of Raoul's annual income would have been $86,000 in 1994. (See p. 3.)

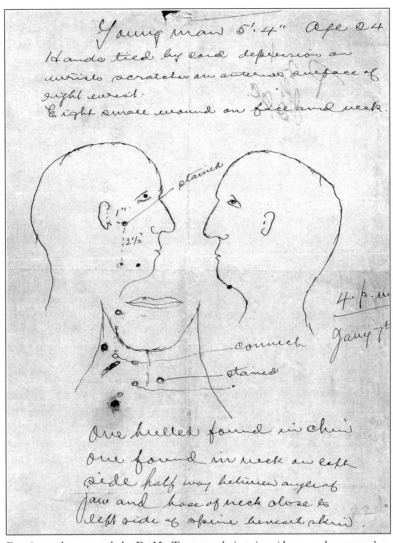

Drawing and notes made by Dr MacTaggart and given in evidence at the coroner's inquest on 9 January 1922.

later, having changed his name by adding "Lajoie," the French equivalent of Farah,* he married Marie Anne Chartré, a sixteen-year-old
French Canadian. Together, they raised ten children. Farah-Lajoie
spoke seven languages. A persistent man, he was a constant thorn in
the side of organized crime and had just finished exposing the under-
world network that had been pillaging the Canadian National and
Canadian Pacific Railway warehouses. He was also credited with
closing down the clandestine gambling dens which had flourished in
the city for many years. Perhaps his most dramatic accomplishment
had been his single-handed prevention of an assassination attempt
against the Papal Delegate at an outdoor Mass during Montreal's 1911
International Eucharistic Congress.

As usual, Farah-Lajoie was given carte blanche in the investigation.
After a short briefing, he drove to the Snowdon toolshed. It was
padlocked and showed no signs of an attempted break-in. The hard-
frozen snow revealed neither footprints nor tire tracks. Because
Farah-Lajoie had been assigned to the case two days after the discovery of the body, he had to rely on Larin for details he would have
preferred to see first hand, such as the position of the body, how it
was dressed, and possible clues in the area. He was able to determine
that there were no signs of a struggle or of the melting effect a warm
body would have had on the frozen snow. He concluded that the
killing had taken place elsewhere.

His next visit was to the morgue to examine the body. Raoul
Delorme had been a muscular and healthy young man 5'4" tall and
weighing about 150 pounds. He had been shot in the head several
times. The bullet holes were small and had closed quickly, with very
little bleeding. Two of the bullets had passed completely through the
head and neck. One of the shots had been fired into the temple at
very close range, the others were in the area of the chin and the neck.
The angle of the bullet wounds indicated that the victim had been
shot from slightly above the right side of his head. He had been either
sitting, kneeling, or bent below his murderer. There were fresh
scratch marks on the back of his right hand and unusually deep
grooves around his wrists. Farah-Lajoie was certain the depth of the
grooves was due to the shrinking effect the freezing temperature had
had on the ropes and that the wrists had been tied to transport the
body rather than to restrain the victim. A larger rope had been found
around his neck. It had been used to tie the two quilts that had
covered his head. Both quilts were stuffed with cotton and flannel

* Farah is the Syrian word for joy, "joie" in French.

and looked homemade. They were stained with what appeared to be dried soap and car grease. A feather was stuck to one of them.

The doctors who performed the autopsy told the detective that two small-calibre bullets had been removed from the victim's chin and jaw. A small portion of bloodstained food had been found in his stomach, but there were no traces of poison, drugs, or alcohol. Raoul's suit was bloodstained, with black powdermarks on the collar. The position of the stains showed that Raoul had bled from the nose and mouth. His overcoat showed no sign of the bullet which had pierced the collar of his jacket. This, plus the smooth clean soles on his brown leather shoes, the fresh polish on their edges, and the absence of overshoes and a hat, suggested the crime had been committed indoors. Returning to the police station, Farah-Lajoie met with Pigeon and Desgroseillers, who briefed him on their visit with Father Delorme.

Farah-Lajoie began his investigation by showing pictures of Raoul to taxi drivers and restaurant owners in the neighbourhood of the Princess Theatre but found no one who had seen him. He concluded that he needed more information, which could only come from Father Delorme. He picked up Pigeon and Desgroseillers and around noon the three of them called at 190 St Hubert St. They were greeted by Father Delorme, who ushered them into his study and formally introduced himself to Farah-Lajoie as Father Adélard Delorme, chaplain for the Public Welfare Service, a nearby home for the needy. The priest offered each of the policemen a cigar before beginning his account. He told them that he shared the house with his three unmarried sisters. One of them, Rosa, 30, was his natural sister. The others, Florence and Lilly, 26 and 27, were his half-sisters and Raoul's natural sisters. All of them had been fathered by Alfred Delorme, a wealthy general contractor who had died in 1916, leaving the house to Raoul. Alfred's third wife, who had had no children, had lived in the same house until recently, when she had left due to illness. Another sister, Claudia, was married to Adélard Tétrault, a bank manager, and lived elsewhere in the city with her husband.

Father Delorme impressed Farah-Lajoie. A charming and rather handsome man of medium size in his mid-thirties, he had brown hair, a good complexion, and a persistent gaze from behind a rimless pince-nez attached to his right ear by an elegant chain. A mint candy seemed to be a permanent fixture in his mouth. He spoke with authority and purpose, using many hand gestures for emphasis, and made it clear that nothing could be done in the household without his prior approval. As the priest rambled on about his family, Farah-Lajoie noticed that he was favouring his right arm and keeping his wrist tucked in the sleeve of his cassock. When the sleeve slipped forward, he noticed a brownish-red welt circling the priest's right wrist. Farah-Lajoie casually asked him if he had hurt his hand and Father Delorme told him that he had slipped on the ice on his way to celebrate Mass that morning and one of the attendants at the Public Welfare Service had applied iodine to his wrist.

When asked about Raoul, the priest said that he was twenty-five years old and had been attending the University of Ottawa for the last five years. He had come home on 22 December for the Christmas break. While home, he had been in the habit of getting up late in the morning and playing records on his new Pathephone phonograph, his favourite hobby. He also enjoyed movies. He added that no one had called on Raoul recently and that he rarely stayed out overnight but had done so at Christmas when, without advance notice, he had spent the night at a friend's home, where he had shared in the traditional *réveillon* after Midnight Mass.* Delorme remembered having reproached him for that. Raoul had no girl friends. Indeed, the priest emphasized that he had introduced his brother to several "honest and pretty Catholic girls" but that nothing had come of it. Raoul's school grades were poor but school officials had reported progress. He was looking forward to returning to college after Epiphany and had just bought a new pair of shoes for his return. His bags were packed, his clothes pressed, and he was ready to leave the morning his body was found. Father Delorme added that the previous Thursday he had sent Raoul to Holy Confession in preparation for Epiphany. As Farah-Lajoie listened, it became increasingly obvious that Delorme had been in total control of Raoul since their father's death. It also seemed clear that he had been very conscientious about his young brother's physical and spiritual welfare. "He's authoritarian," Farah-Lajoie thought to himself, "but he certainly seems unselfish in his dedication to his family and vocation. They're lucky to have him."

His recital over, Father Delorme leaned back in his chair and offered Farah-Lajoie and his assistants mint candies or another cigar. Farah-Lajoie turned down the candies, saying he preferred his own

---

* The *Réveillon de Noël* has its roots in rural Quebec, where a bountiful table of hot food greeted the family on its return from Midnight Mass. It was a welcome sight, considering that many had travelled several miles by horse and buggy in the cold night air and had been fasting all day to prepare for Holy Communion. Often several generations would be present at the festivities, which went on until daybreak. Different family members took turns hosting the *réveillon*.

Pall Mall cigarettes. Before leaving, Farah-Lajoie asked to visit Raoul's room. Father Delorme not only obliged but eagerly offered to show him the whole house. It was a large, rambling, twenty-room house spread over three floors and a basement. The visit started in the study, on the ground floor. The group went through a roomy foyer between the study and the dining room into a large kitchen in the rear of the house. At the back of the kitchen, a door gave access to a long narrow corridor which directed them to two doors leading to the garage. Father Delorme explained that he alone had the key to those two doors and that they were kept locked. Between them was a trap door in the floor and another door which opened onto an outside lane extending to Labelle Street at the rear of the house. The trap door led to the basement. The door from the outside lane was used mostly by the furnace stoker, Ernest Leclerc, who had his own key to allow him to get in and out of the basement without disturbing anyone in the house. Father Delorme lifted the trap door and made his way down to the basement, where there were three rooms, one of which was equipped with three furnaces. The second served as a coal bin and the third as a utility room in which were several piles of ashes. Two small windows looking out onto St Hubert Street provided some light and also served as coal chutes. Farah-Lajoie noticed a door through the common wall which separated the Delorme home from the neighbouring house. He asked about it and was told that it connected with the adjacent basement. The priest explained that the neighbouring house also belonged to Raoul and housed three tenants at 192, 194, and 196 St Hubert Street. It was the classic triplex of that era, made up of three distinct housing units, each on a separate floor with an exclusive entrance from the street. Heating was supplied by a separate furnace system in the other basement. Father Delorme remarked unexpectedly that no foul play could possibly have occurred in the Delorme basement because the neighbours would have heard something.

Delorme led the party back upstairs to the garage and proudly showed off his car. It was a four-passenger Franklin of which, he was quick to point out, there were very few in the city. The garage doors also opened on to the Labelle Street lane. They were locked with a heavy set of vertical steel bars, which Delorme mentioned would have made it impossible for any one to break in. The priest and the policemen then returned to the front of the house, where they climbed a wide semi-circular stairway leading to a large hallway on the second floor. As they were climbing, Desgroselliers mentioned to Farah-Lajoie that on 7 January, when he and Pigeon called on

Delorme, he had noticed some freshly laundered sheets hanging from the bannister. Except for a small sewing room in the back, the second floor had been used solely as Raoul's quarters. It contained a bright and well-furnished double sitting room with a piano and the new Pathephone Raoul had so much enjoyed. This room was separated from Raoul's bedroom by a large bay-windowed alcove that Raoul had used as a study.

The group walked up to the third floor where Father Delorme and his three sisters had their bedrooms. The priest's cupboard contained his religious vestments and several cassocks as well as two cans of ether, one full, the other almost empty.*

Farah-Lajoie asked Father Delorme if he owned a gun. "Yes, I've had one since my father died in 1916," he answered. "It's common knowledge among my friends. I keep it in my car for protection on my trips and during night visits to the sick." Farah-Lajoie asked to see the gun and Delorme led him to the car and pointed to a pocket sewn on the inside of the driver's door. The detective removed a 25-calibre Bayard automatic and a box of bullets. He asked Delorme if he had ever used the gun. "Yes, once – last summer," he said, "I was motoring in the U.S. with Raoul and shot at a dog that was barking at him. Raoul was very timid."

Remembering how clean the soles of Raoul's shoes had been, Farah-Lajoie then asked to see the new overshoes Delorme had mentioned earlier. He was taken to a shoe cupboard near the front door and shown two similar pairs, one of which was new. Looking at the other pair, Farah-Lajoie asked, "Did the older pair belong to Raoul?" Delorme was hesitant about answering, so the detective had him try them on. They didn't fit. When the detective said he would take the old pair to the police station, the priest appeared somewhat disturbed.

Having completed the tour of the house, Farah-Lajoie lit a Pall Mall cigarette and asked Delorme to account for his and Raoul's activities on the day of the murder. The priest ushered the group back to his study, reached into his candy box for a mint, and began. "As usual, I got up at five o'clock and after washing and shaving went to the Public Welfare Service to say my daily seven o'clock Mass.

---

* Ether was first used as an anesthetic in the mid-nineteenth century. But before that it was often used at "ether parties," where the participants inhaled it and went off into "spasms of joyous abandon" as reported in Melvin Harris's *The Book of Firsts* (U.K.: Michael O'Mara books, 1994). Its use as an intoxicant continued until hard drugs, such as cocaine, became easily available. Ice cold ether sprinkled on fresh strawberries was a popular recipe with well-to-do Europeans.

Around eight I walked back home and, it being a holy day of obligation, I awoke Raoul to go to nine o'clock Mass and Communion.
Later, I had breakfast with Raoul and our sisters on their return from
Mass. At eleven, Raoul and I had a talk in his study and at noon we
lunched with Florence and Lilly. Rosa, as usual, ate at Rondeau's, a
French pastry shop a few blocks away on St Denis street. After lunch
I went to my study, where I read my breviary* and worked on some
personal business. Raoul left for the Princess Theatre around half
past two, after having borrowed my gold pocket watch. Before leaving
he asked me for $20,† telling me the $5 he had wouldn't be enough
to pay for his day's entertainment. Around three o'clock I headed back
to the Public Welfare Service for afternoon prayers, returned home
around a quarter to four, and continued working in my study for
another hour. At about five, I picked up my furnace stoker, Ernest
Leclerc, and drove him to one of my properties to check out the
furnace. When he was through, I drove him here to do the same
thing. We arrived around six fifteen. I left him in the basement and
had supper with Florence and Lilly. At seven Raoul telephoned to tell
me he had met some friends who had a car. He said he would be
having a dinner with them "in some style" at a downtown restaurant
and afterwards they were going to the Allan Theatre and for a drive.
He added that if he didn't return that night, he would be back the
next morning. When I asked him if he wouldn't rather invite his
friends home for the evening, Raoul answered, "It's my business. If
I'm not home tonight, I'll be there tomorrow," and hung up. I told
my sisters about Raoul's call and they both seemed concerned. At
eight I headed out to Mr Papillon's jewellery store to get my cousin's
watch which I had left there for repairs. I arrived at the jewellery
store around half past eight and about ten minutes later I returned
home on the St Denis tramway. I got off at the corner of Sherbrooke
street at about a quarter to nine and stopped to chat with Police
Constable Godbout, who was directing traffic at the corner of
St Catherine and St Denis. I got home shortly before nine. Rosa and
Lilly had left with Rosa's boy friend, but Florence was at home with
hers. They left shortly after I got there. From about nine o'clock on
I was alone. Leclerc was working on the furnace when I got home
but he left a few minutes after my arrival. I then went out to the

---

* The breviary, a book of scripture readings and prayers, was compulsory daily reading
for every Roman Catholic cleric. This obligation took one to two hours and failing to
complete it was considered a sin. This obligation lasted until the Second Vatican
Council in the early 1960s.
† $172 in 1994 dollars. (See p. 3.)

garage and worked on my car for about half an hour. At about a quarter after ten I returned to my study to read my breviary. That didn't last long because I felt that the house was cold and went down to the basement to look at the furnace. The fire was out. I must have stayed down there about three hours, cleaning out the furnace, refilling it, and finally getting the coal to burn. At about one o'clock Lilly, who had returned earlier and had been kept awake by the noise in the basement, came to the door and called out, "Aren't you going to bed Adélard? It's past one o'clock." Half an hour or so later I went up to bed, but after about an hour the telephone woke me up. All I could hear at the other end of the line was a plaintive voice calling my name. I tried to find out who was there but couldn't get any answer. I finally hung up. Around three o'clock the phone rang again. I didn't bother to answer until one of my sisters said it might be Raoul. When I did answer, all I heard was the same kind of wailing sound. I hung up. When the same call came through an hour or so later, I asked the operator where the calls were coming from. "A phone booth," she said. I asked her for the number but was told it was against regulations to reveal it. I insisted, telling her I was a priest and didn't want to be bothered any more. She promised not to put any more calls through to my number until morning. I went back to bed and got up shortly afterwards at five to start my day. On my way to say Mass I slipped on the icy sidewalk and sprained my wrist. After returning home around nine, I went to buy some snow chains for my tires. At ten o'clock, I drove to Leclerc's and took him to start the furnace at my Amherst street property. At eleven, I was getting worried and I telephoned my step-mother to tell her about Raoul's absence. It was during that telephone conversation that Officers Pigeon and Desgroseillers came to tell me about having found Raoul's body."

Farah-Lajoie thanked Delorme for the information, complimented him on his thoroughness and asked that he not speak to anyone about the case. When he wondered out loud if Raoul's death might have been a suicide, the priest commented sarcastically that six bullets in the head made such a theory rather far fetched. "I once saved the life of a man who had shot himself four times," Farah-Lajoie replied. He went on to caution Father Delorme about avoiding newspaper reporters and private detectives. The priest agreed but added, "I would like to put an ad in the paper offering a reward of $10,000, $15,000 or even $25,000* to whoever brings my brother's killers to justice. Many

* In 1994, $86,000; $129,000; $215,000 respectively. (See p. 3.)

of my friends have suggested I make such an offer." Farah-Lajoie advised against it, saying it was premature. As the three policemen were on their way out, Father Delorme edged up to Pigeon and Desgroseillers, pointed to Farah-Lajoie and whispered, "I don't like that man's face. I can see in his eyes that he doesn't practice any religion and likes to flirt with women." The two detectives replied that Farah-Lajoie was the best on the force. The visit had lasted almost two hours.

On his return to the station, Farah-Lajoie found a message asking him to call the police chief of Côte St Michel, a north end suburb about ten miles from downtown Montreal known for its active night-life. Someone had found a bloodstained cap in the area around 6:30 A.M. on 7 January and had handed it over to the police. It had been discovered less than a mile from Chez Tremblay and Chez Collerette, two all-night dance halls. The chief added that he had also noticed a small pool of frozen blood near where it had been discovered. Farah-Lajoie rushed to Côte St Michel, but by the time he arrived it was almost dark and a light snow had fallen, making it impossible to locate the bloodstained snow. He decided to postpone his search until the next day, but retrieved the cap. In addition to the bloodstains, he noticed that the fur lining had been torn and the earflaps turned up and tied over the top.

On his way back downtown, Farah-Lajoie dropped in on Father Delorme to see if he could identify the cap. The priest immediately recognized it as the one his brother had been wearing when he left for the movies, "I bought it for him two or three years ago and on the morning he disappeared he asked his sister to sew up the lining." He called his sisters downstairs. Florence confirmed what he said, adding that she had done the sewing. When told that the cap had been found near some bloodstained snow, Father Delorme seemed pleased, commenting, "That's where the murder must have taken place – you have a very good lead there."

Early next morning Farah-Lajoie returned to Côte Saint-Michel to continue searching for the patch of bloodstained snow. He had arranged to be met there by the men who had discovered both it and the cap. Joseph Desjardins, who had reported the discovery to the local police, led him right to the spot. It was about 200 feet off the main road on a well-beaten foot path. Desjardins explained that when he had first seen it, "It was about two feet in diameter and had a hole in the middle, as if the blood had first been poured in and then spread out." The cap had been found later by Ambroise Gravel, who had taken the same route and seen it lying on the road. He had, however, not seen the bloodied patch of snow. Farah-Lajoie felt there was something odd about these discoveries. If there was a connection between the cap and the bloodstained snow, he couldn't see how Desjardins could have missed seeing the cap, which was lying on the road at the end of his path, or how Gravel, who had found the cap, could miss seeing the blood, which he would have had to walk over on his way to the cap. He also wondered why the cap had nothing but a few bloodstains on the visor. He collected some of the bloodied snow and took it downtown for analysis.

Meanwhile, rumours were beginning to circulate about Father Delorme. There was talk that his conduct left much to be desired. Some said that his father had decided to disinherit him and that it was only after recommendations from a friend that he bequeathed something to him, on the proviso that he manage Raoul's assets. Rumour also had it that shortly before his death Raoul had taken out a $25,000 insurance policy on his life and named Adélard as sole beneficiary. There were suggestions that Adélard mixed with a bad crowd and enjoyed the company of rather shady women. Farah-Lajoie noted all this, but tried to keep it in perspective. Here was a priest who lived with three women in a downtown house, drove a Franklin, smoked big cigars, rented out apartments, and transacted business. While this made him vulnerable to malicious tongues, it didn't make him guilty. The detective put the rumours down to anti-Catholic bigots who would seize on anything to criticize the Church.

L'Affaire Delorme dominated the press. On 9 January a front page story in *La Presse*, under the headline "The bloody Snowdon Tragedy," described both the brutality of the crime and the anguish of the priest on the death of his brother. Suggesting that there may have been several killers, *La Presse* reported:

Bandits must have thought the unfortunate victim was carrying a lot of money and committed their cowardly act by shooting him several times. One bullet pierced his throat and another shattered his skull. The thugs emptied his pockets and wrapped his head in a thick cloth to prevent any traces of blood. They then put the body in their car and dropped it off in an area of the city where they knew there would be little night-time traffic … Their attack was ferocious. As mentioned by the forensic surgeon, using a small calibre hand-gun meant they had to fire at their victim seven or eight times, leaving his face riddled with bullets. According to the doctors, death came slowly and it was only when a bullet finally pierced a major artery that the bandits accomplished their diabolical work … One of our reporters visited Father Delorme and found him to be in a state of great anguish. He obviously had a great deal of affection for his departed brother, telling our reporter, "He was an accomplished young man, successful in his studies and with a promising future. When my father died, he entrusted Raoul to me saying, 'I made a man of you, do the same with Raoul.' My only purpose in life was to fulfil the promise I made then. My sincerest wish was to see his hard work and valuable qualities rewarded with a prominent place in society. We have no clues as to the identity of the killers who have plunged our family into such a cruel sorrow."

Delorme had given Farah-Lajoie an open invitation to drop in on him whenever he wanted. After having dropped off the cap at the crime lab, the detective and his colleagues returned to 190 St Hubert. Delorme greeted them exuberantly, singing the lyrics of a popular French Canadian song, *Bonsoir, mes amis, bonsoir*, as he led them into his study. "What's the good news?" he asked. "Has the blood been analysed yet? I'm anxious to hear the results. If it's human blood, I will have been right." Farah-Lajoie lit a cigarette and asked Father Delorme for a copy of his father's will. "Notary Bergeron has it, but I can tell you what it says. Raoul's inheritance consisted of real estate, including this house, which was valued at $65,000 when our father died. He also received $1,000 in cash, free and clear of any obligations. I inherited properties worth $22,000 but had to pay debts of $16,000, $2,500 in funeral expenses, and a monthly annuity of at least $50 to my step-mother.* Today, Raoul's income is more than $10,000 annually and mine is over $6,000. As I have already said, I was responsible for managing his assets and those of my half-sisters Lily and Florence. They can do nothing without my consent. I am the "papa" of this house. I give them everything they require but they have to ask me." The priest confirmed the rumor of the $25,000 insurance policy on Raoul's life, adding that he held another one for $1,000 in the case of death by accident.

"I took good care of Raoul," he said. He went on to talk about how he had nursed Raoul for several months during his convalescence following an appendectomy about a year earlier. "After he got

---

* On the basis of a basket of 487 current goods and services, $12.81 was required in 1994 to buy what $1.00 could buy in 1916. On that basis the above values would have the following purchasing power in 1994:

1916 $	1994 $	1916 $	1994 $
65,000	832,650	16,000	204,960
1,000	12,810	2,500	32,025
22,000	281,820	50	641

better, I took him on a car trip to the United States, I never refused him anything." Farah-Lajoie asked if Raoul had left a will. Delorme answered that he might have written one before his operation. He hadn't seen it and felt it might be with the notary. Farah-Lajoie thanked Delorme for his usual hospitality and he and his colleagues left.

Farah-Lajoie felt that the prevailing theory that Raoul had been killed by thugs could be eliminated – things just didn't point that way. Raoul seemed to have been a rather quiet and shy young man and, although he was financially well off, Father Delorme had administered his affairs with a tight fist and given him very little spending money. He didn't seem the type to have attracted thugs by flashy clothes or an ostentatious display of money. In any event, he had only about $20 when he left home, and much of that would have been spent at the movies and on dinner with his friends. He wondered about those friends. It sounded as if they were also students. What motive would they have had? Certainly not what remained of the $20. What about his family? Could he have been killed at home? It seemed strange that both pairs of his overshoes were there. Why would he have gone out in the cold without them? It didn't seem possible that Raoul's sisters could have been involved. They were well-off, lived comfortably in Raoul's house, and had everything taken care of for them. There was no reason for them to want to change their cosy routine. Rosa's boyfriend, Richard Davis, had been dating her for only four to five months and had never met Raoul. Florence's boyfriend, Ovide Tassé, might have seen Raoul briefly on no more than two or three occasions. Lilly didn't have a boyfriend. Claudia was the wife of a well-respected manager of the Bank of Montreal. She lived elsewhere and was completely outside the sphere of her brothers and sisters. Father Delorme was financially secure in his own right and his relationship with the victim had always been very good. "Besides," Farah-Lajoie thought, "priests don't go around killing people." There was no reason why any of his family would have wanted to kill Raoul. "Could it have been Leclerc, the furnace stoker?" he asked himself. After all, he had a key to the house. "But what would have been the motive?" he thought, "and how could he have taken the body all the way to Snowdon?" From all accounts Leclerc was an illiterate who would not have had the resources to commit such a crime. Farah-Lajoie dismissed that theory. It was clear that he needed more evidence and there was less than a week until the coroner's inquest resumed. He returned to the police station and met with Chief Lepage to discuss his dilemma. They decided to intensify the investigation in Côte St Michel. As he was about to leave the chief's office, the phone rang. A worried Delorme was at the other end of the line. In a state of panic, he summoned the detective to his home. "I have received several anonymous letters and they scare me," he said nervously.

Farah-Lajoie grabbed Sergeant Detective Pigeon and they both rushed to 190 St Hubert. On arrival, they were greeted by a surprisingly calm Delorme, who ushered them to his study as if he had all the time in the world. He casually asked them for an update on things and didn't even mention the anonymous letters until reminded by his visitors. "Oh yes, here they are. What do you think?" The detectives carefully reviewed them. Many volunteered information, others were notes of condolences accompanied by Mass offerings. A few, obviously sent by cranks, contained vulgar insults. Farah-Lajoie didn't attach any importance to them.

The next day Farah-Lajoie and his assistants combed the restaurants, taverns, hotels, and clubs, showing pictures of Raoul wherever they went. No one they spoke to recognized him or remembered having seen any unusual traffic in that neighbourhood on the night of the murder. The detectives also inquired in the Snowdon area, where a late evening social function had been held on 6 January at St Matthew's Anglican Church. Many members of the congregation were questioned, but none remembered having seen anything unusual on either their way to or from the church, which was located about 100 yards from the toolshed. The police also met with the prefect of discipline of Ottawa University, who was in Montreal to attend Raoul's funeral. He was unable to provide any useful information, but confirmed that the victim had been popular in college, although he didn't seem to have any intimate friends.

Farah-Lajoie was frustrated by the constant dead ends. For lack of a better idea he returned to 190 St Hubert Street, where Raoul's wake was being held. Newspaper coverage of the crime had attracted many people to the Delorme home and Farah-Lajoie hoped that he might pick up some additional leads. At this point, he thought, anything would help. When Father Delorme saw him arrive, he led him into his study and begged him to attend Raoul's funeral next day, "in case the murderers decide to show up at it." Farah-Lajoie promised he and his two assistants would be there and asked to see Raoul's will at the notary's office. "I think he left his will in Ottawa," Delorme replied, adding, "I hope he didn't forget me in it. I've been very good to him." With that the priest excused himself and joined some visitors who had come to pay their respects. As Farah-Lajoie watched him graciously accepting condolences, it struck him that he had never seen Father Delorme out of his cassock, even in the privacy of his own home on Farah-Lajoie's unannounced visits.

A crowd of nearly 2,000 attended the funeral service at Saint-Jacques Church on Wednesday, 11 January. Father Delorme had arranged that everyone be given a candle and asked that they be held high during a Requiem High Mass which, except for a momentary outburst of tears, he sang with great flourish. Farah-Lajoie noticed that even while accepting condolences at the church door after the service, he kept an eye out for photographers. He even found an opportunity to be photographed with one of the detectives, telling him, "Tomorrow we'll both be in the newspaper." He then led an impressive funeral procession to Côte des Neiges Cemetery, where Raoul's remains were deposited in a holding vault pending burial after the spring thaw. Throughout the ceremony, Farah-Lajoie kept his eyes open for anything suspicious. Although he didn't notice anything, that afternoon's late edition of the *Montreal Daily Star* ran a story under the headline "Conversation at Delorme Funeral May Provide Clue." The conversation referred to was reported as having taken place between three men standing on the sidewalk in front of the Delorme home on St Hubert Street as the funeral cortege was forming. "Better not stay here too long," said one of them to the other two. "We better not smoke now. Let's not stay around here too long, its not safe." The story went on to state that the conversation was reported to the police.

Meanwhile, reports were pouring in to the police station. Someone claimed to have seen a person fitting Raoul's description telephoning from a restaurant at the corner of St Catherine and University streets on the evening of the murder and then getting into an automobile with two men. Another had apparently sighted a large, highpowered car speeding along St Catherine Street at about seven o'clock the same evening. He claimed that it had had three passengers, one of whom was seated in the back with his head wrapped in a blanket. It was also claimed that a car had been seen in the early morning of 7 January close to where the body was found. The car in all three reports fit the same description. One report took Farah-Lajoie 125 miles away to Ottawa, where a garage attendant reported that a large, mud-spattered car fitting the description had been left with him by a suspicious-looking stranger. It turned out the car belonged to a farmer who lived in the outlying district. While in Ottawa Farah-Lajoie called on officials at the University of Ottawa in hopes of finding out more about Raoul's will. He learned that Raoul had signed a will in

February 1921, before his operation. He had left it in the custody of a school official, an Oblate priest, who had returned it to him before he travelled to Montreal for the Christmas break. When asked if he knew the will's contents, the official answered that he didn't. He said that Raoul's conduct at college had been above reproach and that he had been absent only one afternoon in the current term.

On his return to Montreal Farah-Lajoie was informed by Sergeant Detective Pigeon that Father Delorme had recently visited a gunsmith by the name of Oscar Haynes. He immediately went to the gunsmith's shop, taking with him the Bayard handgun and bullets he had taken from Father Delorme's car. Haynes told him the priest was a regular customer who often brought in his pistol for service and repair. He had last seen him on 27 December when Delorme had come to the shop and traded an old 32-calibre Iver Johnson for the 25-calibre Bayard. He had also bought two boxes of twenty-five steel bullets. Farah-Lajoie showed Haynes the Bayard and bullet boxes. After checking its serial number, Haynes confirmed that it was the gun he had exchanged for the Iver Johnson. He also identified the bullets, adding, however, that the 25-calibre Bayard was a very common gun and that there were thousands of them in the city. Farah-Lajoie asked if he could make some tests in Haynes' firing range. The gunsmith agreed. They took a Bayard, a Browning, and a Mauser off the shelf, all of the same calibre as Father Delorme's Bayard. Out of each pistol they fired a bullet taken from the box Haynes' had sold to Delorme. A fourth bullet was fired from Delorme's Bayard. Farah-Lajoie took all four bullets to the crime lab.

The 27 December date of Father Delorme's visit to the gun shop struck Farah-Lajoie as odd. It didn't fit with what Delorme had told him about having had the handgun since his father's death five years earlier. Had the priest been lying to him? Not knowing the answer bothered him and he decided he would have to pursue his investigation of the Delorme family further. He wanted to talk to Raoul's sisters, but the priest's constant presence seemed to be shielding them. He also wanted to go through the Delorme house alone, without the priest as a guide. He had to find a way to get him out of the house. His problem would be solved if he could convince the coroner to issue a warrant for Father Delorme's arrest. However, it was highly unlikely that the coroner would do this because of a hunch, and the priest's only suspicious behaviour so far was his apparent lie about the gun. But Farah-Lajoie decided to try. With that in mind, he went back to the police station and thoroughly reviewed the evidence, neatly itemizing possible motives.

Alone in the stillness of his office, he lit a Pall Mall and jotted down all possible motives for the crime: espionage, vengeance, theft, madness, and personal gain. He eliminated the first. Raoul was not associated with any of the many radical or secret societies generally referred to as "anarchists" and therefore could not be involved in any espionage.* Vengeance was also ruled out. Except for his stays in Ottawa during school semesters, Raoul remained close to home and had no romantic involvements. The possibility of jealousy or of a romantic triangle did not exist. Farah-Lajoie took the idea of theft as a motive more seriously. However, Raoul was not widely known to be rich in either Ottawa or Montreal. He might have spoken about his fortune to some of his classmates, but was not a big spender. Indeed, he had the reputation of being stingy. Farah-Lajoie thought of the fake money and of Raoul's seven o'clock phone call on the evening of his murder. Could the murderers have been the friends he had run into? They were probably students, he thought, and since fake money was in rather common usage as a teaching aid in colleges, they would have recognized it as such. But neither $20 nor a gold watch would justify shooting several bullets into a person, tying up the body, taking the time to meticulously wrap it up, fasten it with dozen safety pins, find a car, a driver, and get to Snowdon by way of Côte St Michel. He wondered about the gold pocket watch. Could someone have possibly killed for it? Maybe it held the answer, but he didn't think so. If theft was the motive, it didn't seem possible it had been committed by Raoul's friends, which left the possibility that it was a professional job. Farah-Lajoie couldn't accept that theory either. Professionals used larger calibre pistols, left their victims where they shot them, and didn't bother to wrap up the body with the same care a child would use to wrap up a doll.

Had Raoul been the victim of a madman? The detective quickly rejected that theory. Maniacs kill on sudden impulse and, because they often don't realize what they have done, make no attempt to flee or

---

* Concern about radical groups was not uncommon in the early part of the twentieth century. In 1918, shortly after World War I began, Germany started setting up espionage and sabotage bases in North America, leading to fear of enemy aliens. The Russian Revolution also exported the "Big Red Scare" to this continent and the Catholic Church was active in condemning all Socialist Communists. As well, there was a great deal of social unrest. Labour unions were in their formative years, and new beliefs were challenging the ruling class. The more militant groups, who resorted to violence, were generally called "anarchists." There were riots, murders, bombings, vigilantie groups, and private militias. As is the case today, a college campus was a popular recruiting area for many of these movements, so it was therefore not unexpected that Farah-Lajoie would include espionage on his list of possibilities.

hide their deed. They are very quickly discovered, sometimes on the spot. That left only personal gain – and the person with the most to gain financially from Raoul's death was Father Delorme. He would receive the $25,000 insurance proceeds and probably inherit all of Raoul's rental properties.

His carefully prepared notes gave Farah-Lajoie some confidence in his theory. Perhaps he could persuade the coroner to issue an arrest warrant. Arresting Father Delorme would allow him more freedom in his investigation and might even provoke a confession. But by this time it was late evening. Should he go to Coroner McMahon now or wait until morning? He decided to go immediately and called on the coroner at his home. McMahon reviewed the material carefully and concluded that he needed more evidence. His reaction was understandable. A seventy-year-old devout Irish-Catholic, born and raised in the Province of Quebec, who had followed his Cours Classique at the Séminaire de Ste-Thérèse and spent his spare time as choir master at l'Église St-Joseph, the Notre-Dame Basilica, and the Montreal Cathedral, he no doubt found it almost inconceivable that a priest could be suspected of murder. Although sympathetic to Farah-Lajoie's theory, he stressed that because a member of the clergy was involved he would have to insist on ironclad evidence. "Can you imagine how much controversy a warrant would cause," he asked? "Every priest and nun in the Province would want our heads." Dejected, Farah-Lajoie headed home. But despite his failure to get a warrant, his meeting with the coroner had been productive: in explaining his theory to McMahon, he had convinced himself that Delorme was the killer. Soon that thought would become an obsession.

Next morning, front-page newspaper stories reported a $10,000* reward offered by Father Delorme for information leading to the arrest and conviction of the murderers. The announcement had been made at a press conference he had called to congratulate the police on their work and Delorme had suggested that the reward might be increased if nothing came of the original offer. Drawing attention to the missing gold pocket watch, he said it had been ripped from his brother's vest and pointed out that the initials "A.D." engraved on its back would make it easy to identify. He added "If you can find that watch, it will lead you to the killer."

Meanwhile coroner McMahon had ordered Raoul's body to be brought to the morgue for further analysis of the stomach. He was looking for drugs or other soporifics. On 15 January the police

---

* $86,000 in 1994 dollars. (See p. 3.)

reported that a handgun of the same calibre as the one used to kill Raoul had been found in Côte St Michel. Later that day Father Delorme held another press conference, this time to complain that the police were withholding information from him as he hadn't been told about the gun being found. He added "The handgun affair does not seem important to me. I had a handgun which I kept in my car and showed to the detectives on 9 January. It's a gun I've had since my father's death. My father also had one. I always kept mine in the car. I'm frequently called out at night and it's always better to have that kind of protection. I used to take long automobile trips with my brother in the summer and we seldom stopped at a hotel or at a friend's home but slept in the car. The handgun was useful and several times I had to use it to scare away tramps. I also fired several practice shots with it when I first got it. Since then I've kept it well oiled and cleaned."

When asked about the rumours connecting him with the murder, he replied, "It's a hard enough blow for any man to lose his brother under such circumstances without the added weight of being a suspect. Is it reasonable to think that I would kill him for money when I have plenty of my own? Besides, why would I kill him here during the Christmas holidays when I would have ample opportunity in the summer when he and I were often far away in the woods together? We used to sleep far from any town or city and if I were inclined to commit that kind of crime, I could have done it then. People seem to find it strange that I am not connected with any parish and live with my three sisters. I can explain that. When my father died I was in a parish outside Montreal. I asked the bishop to allow me to come to Montreal to be nearer my family and to administer my father's estate. This was granted and I was given a parish in the city. Later the management of the estate demanded so much of my time that I asked to be given a post where I could have more time to myself. My request was granted and now I'm chaplain for the Public Welfare Service. I visit the aged and the sick. I administer the Sacraments and the Last Rites to the dying. I say my daily Mass at St Jacques Church and often help out there. I am always ready to be called upon for help anywhere. There has certainly been no reprimand from the bishop. A member of his staff visited me a short time ago and no reprimand or anything of that nature was mentioned. The detectives have verified that."

Feeling that he had to comment about the newspaper reports that his brother's life insurance would come to him, he made a rather surprising statement, "17 December was my thirty-seventh birthday and I received a birthday card from the president of La Sauvegarde Assurance, with whom I was insured. The next day I called on him to thank him and was met by my agent, Mr Larocque, and Mr Ducharme, secretary of the company. That's when the question of insurance on Raoul's life came up. We first talked of $5,000 to $10,000 coverage but Mr. Larocque, who knew the family, suggested $25,000.*

Adélard Delorme's impromptu statements and his willingness to make them made for great newspaper reading and helped transform a local crime into a national "cause célèbre." His high profile involvement in the case made him a source of great interest to the media, as did his position as a priest. Many Roman Catholics felt he was being unfairly targeted by anti-Catholic factions such as the Freemasons. Others disagreed and felt he was escaping arrest only because he was a priest.

Delorme continued to keep in constant touch with the police department. In addition to the several visits from Farah-Lajoie, he often had telephone conversations with Chief Lepage about how the investigation was going and also visited him at the police station several times. Delorme had taken a liking to Lepage, who had somehow gained the priest's confidence. The same certainly couldn't be said of Farah-Lajoie.

The second session of the Coroner's inquest, held on Tuesday, 17 January, wasn't much longer than the first. Adélard Delorme was the only witness. Coroner McMahon reassured him by explaining that he had been asked to appear because McMahon wanted to ask him about some of the statements he had made to the press. "Rumours about you are far from charitable," he said and asked if the newspaper had correctly reported what he had said. The priest answered it had, except that his automobile had been wrongly reported to be a Ford instead of a Franklin. McMahon remembered the conflicting stories about the handgun and asked Father Delorme if he had owned it since his father's death. Casually nursing his ever-present mint candy, the priest explained that he had exchanged it in December. The handgun the detectives had was the new one. He admitted that he had not explained that detail previously. The coroner asked about the value of his father's estate. Delorme said he doubted it was worth $185,000† as had been claimed by the press. He added, contrary to what he had previously told police, that he had received $20,000 in cash and Raoul had received $10,000. Asked if he would accept being audited, the

* $215,000 in 1994 dollars. (See p. 3.)
† $2,370,000 in 1994 dollars. (See p. 19.)

priest answered that he would if it would be of help to the inquiry. After having assured the priest that he would not issue such an order unless it was absolutely necessary, the coroner adjourned until 24 January. McMahon was obviously handling the inquest with great caution, possibly feeling intimidated by the publicity.

As soon as he left the room Father Delorme rushed to speak to reporters. It was unclear whether he was attempting to make himself look better to the public or searching for a support system that could help him in his grief. Whatever the reason, he was a sad and amusing as well as somewhat disturbing figure, standing in his cassock, sucking on his mints, his attitude shifting from docile resignation to aggressive anger. "It hurts my feelings to see my name dragged in the mud. How could anyone suppose that I would kill my brother for $25,000 when I have enough assets of my own? We must find the murderers! When that happens I will demand that, to set an example, punishment be carried out in the Mount Royal Arena, whatever the price! I want revenge for my brother's blood. The diabolical rumours must be stopped. We must silence those detractors who are spewing insults and abuse on everyone. They can be found even in high society. But who are they? Free thinkers, atheists, anticlerical people, policemen, vain men – in a word bad citizens. We must see that their names are revealed."

Father Delorme's statements, the police's inability to come up with hard evidence, and a second postponement of the inquest increased the split in public opinion. The case had become the main topic of conversation almost everywhere and the priest acquired quite a following. Although the Catholic Church didn't take an official stand, many parish priests in the archdiocese of Montreal supported Father Delorme from the pulpit, reminding their flock of the ninth commandment, "Thou shalt not bear false witness against thy neighbour." Some even suggested it might be sinful for a Roman Catholic to think that an ordained priest could be a murderer. Anonymous letters were pouring into the coroner's office, the police department, and the newspapers. They were almost evenly divided between those who supported the priest and those who felt he was guilty. Some were critical of Farah-Lajoie. Some threatened Father Delorme. There were prayers and poems to the memory of Raoul. Several writers provided "important" leads, all of which were followed and all of which proved false. The priest's offer of a $10,000 reward not only created a great deal of interest among private detectives but also brought out an array of fortunetellers and palmists who, for an appropriate fee, guaranteed to deliver the murderer or murderers.

The police seemed to have reached a dead end, although they stated that they were still looking for a city cab driver who might have some information and also for a student from the University of Ottawa who was reported to have met the victim a few hours before his death. Many people saw these searches as nothing more than delaying tactics. Pressure was beginning to be felt at higher levels and at the request of the attorney general the provincial police were brought into the case. The consensus in police circles continued to be that the murder had been committed in Côte St-Michel and the body driven to Snowdon. It was suggested that the number of bullets pointed to a drugged maniac as the killer.

Meanwhile, Father Delorme continued to keep a high public profile. He made another public declaration, stating that Raoul's will was in Ottawa but that he neither knew of its contents nor was interested in finding out until the mystery had been cleared up. He repeated his plea for help from all Montrealers in capturing the killers.

On Thursday, 19 January, a story in *La Presse* stated that the police were on the verge of a breakthrough. Chief Lepage was quoted as saying, "We expect very positive developments in the Delorme case. Within twenty-four hours we expect to give important information to the coroner and it is now almost certain that when the inquest resumes next Tuesday we will be in a position to proceed." When asked if he had any particular theory, he replied, "My feeling is that there must have been at least two bandits because every indication is there was a terrible struggle between the murderers and the student." A few days later the *Toronto Globe* reported that "those prominent in the case firmly believe that an arrest is only a few days off. Some stated today that one had actually taken place but the police deny arresting anyone. Speculation is rife concerning the outcome of tomorrow's adjourned inquest. Many people are of the opinion that it will terminate with the arrest of somebody."

When the adjourned coroner's inquest resumed on 24 January it was virtually besieged by curious onlookers. The hallways and staircases were so crowded that it was impossible to get into the hearing room, leaving the authorities no choice but to evacuate the building except for lawyers and reporters. Under pressure from the coroner's remarks at the two previous sessions, the police had found more evidence. Some fifteen witnesses, including the Delorme sisters, were to be heard. They were told to wait in the hallway until individually escorted into the inquest room as each was called.

Ernest Leclerc, the furnace stoker, testified he had spent about one hour in the basement on 6 January, between about six and seven P.M.

and had found the furnace to be working well. He reported that he had returned early the next morning and found that although the furnace was full of warm coal it wasn't generating any heat.

A neighbour then took the stand and said that at eleven o'clock that same evening he had heard the roar of Father Delorme's car engine in the garage, but couldn't tell whether it was entering or leaving. Later, at about one A.M., he was awakened by the sound of coal being shaken in the Delorme furnace and the voice of a woman shouting, "Aren't you going to bed, Adélard?"

Ovide Tassé and Richard Davis, the Delorme sisters' boyfriends, were also heard, but couldn't provide any information about possible foul play. Although the names of the two men had come up a few times since the case began, this was their first public appearance and many people were curious to see what they looked like. As the two men rushed from the building, trying to shield their faces, a murmur ran through the crowd gathered outside as an onlooker shouted, "One of them is a negro."

The main attraction of the inquest was the Delorme sisters. A nervous Florence Delorme was the first to take the stand. Wearing a well-tailored coat with a fur collar and matching muff, she was a dull-looking girl who wore thick eyeglasses and seemed rather slow-witted. Among other things, she identified Raoul's cap and overshoes, adding she was sure he had put them on before leaving the house on the afternoon of the sixth. Her vague testimony, her contradictory statements, and her nervous looks towards her brother finally led Coroner McMahon to tell her that, while he understood that her brother had a great deal of influence on her and she seemed to take his word as Gospel, he didn't want to hear what she had been told, or what she thought she had been told, but only what she had seen and what she knew from personal experience. He reminded her that she was under oath.

McMahon then took Florence through part of her testimony and again asked her if she was absolutely sure Raoul was wearing his overshoes when he left home. She insisted he was. Since the detectives had not found any overshoes on the victim's body and both pairs had been found at the house by Farah-Lajoie, the coroner simply shook his head, looked up at the ceiling, and loudly asked no one in particular how the overshoes could have come back home on their own. His sarcasm was too much for Florence, who broke down and cried. The coroner granted her request to be excused from further testimony.

Lilly then took the stand. Although rather unattractive, she, too, was very well dressed. A heavy-set woman with coarse features, she had a stubborn and ignorant look. On being sworn in, she dissolved into tears. After a few moments she regained her composure, but her testimony failed to help. This left Rosa. Unlike her half-sisters, she was slender, comparatively attractive, and did not appear to be as dull-witted. Her testimony was brief. Proudly, she stated that the priest had been out all evening and she knew nothing else. She refused to testify any further and the coroner was forced to dismiss her.

By this time it had become apparent that there was no clear picture of how much time Father Delorme had spent at home on the evening of the sixth. On his own account, he had been there all evening except for some time between eight and nine. Each of the three Delorme girls told a different story: Florence first said the priest went out at 8:30 but then changed that to 10:30, Lilly said he was in all evening, Rosa said he was out all evening. There was also the conflict between Leclerc's testimony that he worked on the Delorme furnace between six and seven o'clock and the priest's earlier statement that the stoker was still working on it at nine o'clock. Instead of resolving issues, the inquest had only added to the confusion. McMahon adjourned until 31 January.

On the afternoon of 24 January the analysis of Raoul's stomach was made public. It showed no drugs. Digestion had been completed before death. If Raoul's alleged seven o'clock telephone call to his brother when he told him he was about to eat dinner was accepted, allowing for the normal digestive process placed the time of the murder at about ten o'clock. A further report was published on the analysis of the bloodstained snow found at Côte St Michel. The stains turned out to be horse urine. Following on the heels of the confusing coroner's inquest that morning, the report made the whole affair begin to look like a comedy of errors.

A report published in *La Presse* of information from a shipchandler, Michael Barry, directed attention toward the Port of Montreal. One of the largest seaports in the world and second only to New York in North America, the Port of Montreal was equipped to load and unload huge numbers of ships and had simultaneously berthed as many as fifty-six vessels. It was recognized as the greatest grain exporting harbour in the world and had the largest cold storage plants in North America. All of this was even more remarkable considering that it was 1,000 miles inland and yet closer to the port of Liverpool than any port along the eastern seaboard of the U.S., making it one of the cornerstones of intercontinental sea commerce with North America. Except for the Hudson Bay route, its location also made it the closest seaport to the American midwest.

The port was accompanied by a large cast of the type of characters usually associated with portside activities. Although the servicing of ships slowed down when the ice took over during the winter, activity shifted to loading up with supplies and repairing equipment in preparation for the next shipping season. Night life also continued and, with fewer sailors around, the clubs and taverns were more available to Montrealers.

At the time, Montreal had the most active night life in the northeast. The end of the Great War and the introduction of prohibition in the United States had helped the city become a mecca for those who wanted the best in wine, women, and song. The St Lawrence Street area, between St Catherine and Craig in the heart of Montreal, was a world-renowned red-light district. Many outlying areas, such as Côte St Michel, also catered to pleasure seekers. Police tolerance, and in some cases complicity, allowed dance halls, clubs, and cafés to stay open all night despite municipal by-laws. Gambling dens flourished. Train junkets were organized from the large northeastern cities of the United States to take thousands to the "wet" city of Montreal for a weekend of fun. The roaring twenties were beginning and many well-known American radio and nightclub entertainers started their careers in Montreal only to return to the United States with the repeal of prohibition.

Michael Barry reported having seen a man trying to dump a large body-like object in the St Lawrence River in the early morning of 6 January. On seeing Barry, the man pushed the object back in the car and sped away. *La Presse* reported that another witness had seen a car speeding west on St Catherine Street around two o'clock that morning with what appeared to be a corpse in the back seat. At that time the city had only about 250 miles of city roads and a handful of automobiles, most of which were stored during the winter months to avoid engine freezing and treacherous roads during the spring thaw.* With so little car traffic, it was not unreasonable to conclude that it might well have been the same car.

Father Delorme was delighted and called Narcisse Arcand, the reporter from *La Presse* who had broken the story. "We've got them," he said. "You're going to get rich. You found it, you've got the right lead, the detectives haven't come up with anything ... But you found

---

* In the spring of 1922 the *Montreal Daily Star* wrote the following about Montreal roads: "To drive over them in an automobile or hack is positive torture, to cross even the most frequented is to risk limb and possibly life by tripping over deep ruts and gaping holes."

an intelligent lead. So you're going to get the $10,000 reward." His delight with Arcand changed to anger a few days later when the reporter wrote another story suggesting that the priest might be the murderer. Father Delorme summoned Arcand to his house, led him into his den, locked the door behind them and menacingly told his terrified guest, "So now you're starting to make problems for me. You're not so stupid looking, so don't make yourself so detestable. Look at me properly. Don't be afraid. Look at me. What do you think of me? Do I look insane?" When Arcand told him he didn't, Father Delorme handed him a cigar saying, "Smoke this. Now I'm going to give you a story and you're going to publish it. Your stories are starting to harm me. I have friends at *La Presse* and if you and I don't get along you're going to be in trouble." His tone was as pedantic as it was authoritative. Throughout his lengthy monologue he continually referred to the importance of his priesthood and of the Church. He finished by demanding that the crime not be discussed in the presence of children because it could cause the loss of vocations to the priesthood.

Meanwhile some newspapermen developed a new theory, this one triggered by the unfounded rumour that a table napkin with a cigarette burn had been found on Raoul's body. The press quickly linked the napkin with the Orpheum theatre's new burlesque show through the bogus money found on the body. The show had opened on 1 January 1922 and featured three dancers who used bogus money in their act. The dancers were returning to New York on 7 January and, according to some undisclosed sources, Raoul had befriended several people who decided to organize a going-away party for the dancers after their show on 6 January. The murder would have been committed either during or after the party. *La Presse* suggested this connection was borne out by the bogus money, the napkin, and the feminine way in which his coat had been fastened with safety pins. The small calibre gun also pointed to a woman as the killer. *La Presse* concluded that Father Delorme had been unjustly suspected and unfairly treated. The foreign press, which had been closely following the story, also adopted that theory. As early as 10 January the *Times* of London had reported that "it is believed that Delorme was murdered in Montreal and the body taken in a sleigh to the lonely shed where it was discovered. Detectives suggest that Delorme was murdered by a woman for revenge."

There was one constant element in all the proposed theories: Raoul's murderers had stolen a gold watch engraved with "A.D. le 17 décembre." Finding the watch would lead to the killers. A thorough search of the city's pawnshops and other similar establishments, however, had been unsuccessful.

On Thursday, 26 January, Farah-Lajoie decided once again to visit the Delorme house. This time he wanted to take a closer look at Delorme's car. Perhaps the recent Barry report and other stories about late night speeding cars in downtown Montreal had suddenly triggered his interest in it. In any event, he brought along Chief Lepage, whose presence might help relieve any tension between him and the priest. After his usual courteous greeting, Father Delorme led the policemen to the garage, reminding them that "no one is allowed in here without my permission." Inside the car they found two bloodstained cushions and four cardboard boxes covered with chicken feathers. They also noticed two oil-stained blankets on the floor. The priest explained, "Those chicken feathers come from live chickens I got in the country for a friend of mine. The foot blankets belonged to my parents and I sometimes use them as I did on my last trip with Raoul. Blood. What blood? I don't see any blood." Everything was taken to the police station for analysis. The next day, Farah-Lajoie received the crime lab report on the stained cushions. The stains were from human blood. Perhaps, finally, there had been a breakthrough.

Given the new evidence, Farah-Lajoie decided to return immediately to the Delorme home, this time accompanied by Dr Wilfrid Derome, the forensic surgeon. A distinguished-looking man in his mid-forties, Derome was professor of forensic medicine and of toxicology at l'Université de Montréal and the North American pioneer of forensic pathology, which he had studied at the Université de Paris under the famous Dr Balthazard, medico-legal expert for the Sûreté de Paris. In 1914 Derome had founded the Montreal Laboratory of Forensic Medicine, the first of its kind in North America, of which he was the director.* His expertise was not restricted to forensic medicine, where he was considered to be the best in the world. He had also developed the science of ballistics and was equally well

---

* Originally known as Laboratoire de recherche médico-légale et de police technique, it was the third crime laboratory in the world, the two first being in France (Paris, 1868, and Lyon, 1910). The Montreal crime lab inspired the creation of the Chicago equivalent (the Northwestern University Crime Laboratory) which was founded in 1929 as a result of St Valentine's day massacre. It wasn't until November 1932, after J. Edgar Hoover had twice visited Derome and his facility in Montreal, that the FBI started its own. The RCMP followed suit in Regina in 1937. Today, there are well over two hundred forensic medicine facilities on the North American continent. Montreal's remains one of the best.

respected as a handwriting expert. His opinion in all three of those areas carried enormous weight in the courts.*

Although Delorme seemed nervous at seeing a new person involved in the investigation, he led the police to the garage. Dr Derome inspected the car and had the seats brought to his crime lab. Farah-Lajoie also checked the basement again and took away a piece of rope he found that was similar to the one that had held the blanket around Raoul's head. As the police left with this additional material, they told the priest they would also have to take his car away for inspection. Father Delorme sarcastically replied, "Every day you take something out of here. At the end I suppose it will be my turn to go."

The report from the crime lab the next morning showed that an attempt had been made to remove human blood from the rear seat of the car. The soap residue on the seat was identical with the soap stains on the quilts found around Raoul's head and the oil stains on the quilts matched the stains on the two blankets taken from the Delorme garage. The workmanship of the quilts and blankets showed they had been made by the same person. Farah-Lajoie was now sure he could convince the coroner to issue a warrant for Father Delorme's arrest.

However, when he made his request Coroner McMahon told him once again that more evidence would be required. It was now obvious that the coroner wanted irrefutable proof before he would participate in the arrest. He went so far as to adjourn his inquest indefinitely. This decision caused comment not only in police circles but also with the public and even with Father Delorme. The police department, particularly Farah-Lajoie, were accused of either "cowardice and partiality" or "sacrilege and persecution." Many pressed to have Delorme arrested, while others wanted the police and the press to stop harassing him. Embarrassing questions were asked in the legislature. The leader of the opposition accused the police of indiscretion and the press of sensationalism and demanded that the attorney general end what he considered to be a scandalous affair. Even Father Delorme was beginning to show signs of stress. Following the last session of the coroner's inquest, a twenty-four hour police watch had been set up at his house. He was virtually under house arrest. Despite that, he managed to maintain his contact with the press and called another press conferences to state that he wasn't impressed with recent police reports about the bloodstains found on the car cushion. The reason,

---

* In 1920 Dr Derome published *La Médecine légale*, a study on forensic medicine which is still cited before the courts today. In 1929 he published *Expertise en Armes à Feu*, a complete study of firearms and ballistics, also highly acclaimed.

he said, was that he had cut his finger while doing car repairs. "And why haven't they found my watch yet?" he asked, "I'm certain it's in a pawnshop somewhere – and with all that engraving on it, surely someone would notice. And what about my raccoon coat? They've even taken that down to the police station. I have another fur coat, but the one they took is my favourite and I'd like to have it back this winter." He scoffed at police denials that they had taken his coat and became annoyed when questioned about discrepancies in the testimony of several witnesses, saying that there was no difference in the substance of the testimonies. Reacting to a 28 January story in the *Toronto Globe* that he had mortgaged the 190 St-Hubert Street house to cover horsebetting losses in New Orleans, he insisted, "I have never been to New Orleans in my life and have never played the horses anywhere." Finally he angrily ushered the reporters out, saying, "I forbid you to repeat a word of what I've told you." He rambled on incoherently "You've heard nothing and you've asked me nothing. In fact, I didn't listen to you, as my mind was elsewhere. Now mark my words. There is a detective here who heard everything we said. If you repeat a word, I'll have you arrested in the morning." He seemed to have lost all self control.

On 30 January, an interesting development came out of London. It concerned the mysterious phone calls Delorme had said he received during the night of January 6 to 7. The London *Times* reported that the telephone company had said there were no such calls on record.

On Wednesday, 1 February, Father Delorme tried to arrange a meeting with the attorney general of Quebec, Louis-Alexandre Taschereau.* He drafted a letter to him and then telephoned him in the hope of reading the letter to either the attorney general or his assistant. Surprisingly, he was put through. "Mr Attorney General," he read, "this is Father Delorme from Montreal, half-brother of the late Raoul Delorme, killed on the night of the sixth to the seventh of January. I am sorry to disturb you but I would appreciate it if you would listen to me for about five minutes. I am taking the liberty of calling you because for the last three weeks I have been under suspicion by the public and by officers of your department of a terrible accusation which has affected my family, the clergy, to which I belong, and myself. It seems to me that by now a decision should have taken either for or against me. What I am making is a petition for justice. I ask that either the full severity of the law be

---

* Louis-Alexandre Taschereau was also the premier of Quebec. He held both positions until 1936.

directed against me or I be completely exonerated of the outrageous suspicions directed at me as soon as possible. Let justice be done immediately. The Coroner's inquest has been adjourned indefinitely. In the meantime, what happens to my reputation? Does justice have the right to throw me as fodder to the press and the public, who seem to love sensationalism? Everyone seems to want to make this a religious issue. I insist, Mr Attorney General, that this investigation be terminated without further delay, one way or the other, but in accordance with your righteousness, your judgment, and your wisdom. I am satisfied with the conscientious work which your officers are doing in this mysterious case. But for Heaven's sake please finish hounding me from every angle. When you next come to Montreal I'll be happy to see you. My sincere thanks for the attention I know you will give my case." The attorney general replied politely that he would give Father Delorme's request the utmost consideration and thanked him for his call.

Father Delorme also called the press to ask them to publish a further statement.

I request permission from the newspapers to categorically deny the slander that the public seems to enjoy spreading about me.

1 I deny having gone to the Bishop of Montreal to obtain the help of the diocesan authorities.
2 I also deny having gone to see Chiefs Lepage and Bélanger with the diocesan authorities.
3 I deny having used money to buy silence anywhere.
4 I deny having had an interview with any judge, lawyer, or magistrate.
5 Finally, I declare that I have carried out meticulously all of the duties of my ministry.

Things began to move at a faster pace. The attorney general summoned Coroner McMahon and Chief Lepage to Quebec City to meet with him and Chief Dieudonné Lorrain, head of the provincial police. After reviewing the evidence, Taschereau instructed the coroner to reopen his inquest on 14 February and ordered an audit of the Delorme estate books. He also appointed Joseph Charles Walsh, KC,* as special Crown prosecutor. Walsh was a fifty-four-year-old

---

* KC are the initials for King's Counsel, a title conferred on a barrister of distinction appointed to serve as counsel for the Crown. Before 1920, a KC could not be employed in any cause against the Crown (e.g., in defending a prisoner) without special license. When a Queen holds the Crown, the barristers are known as QC for Queen's Counsel.

Roman Catholic Irishman whose background included a brief stay in the House of Commons and an earlier career as a newspaper reporter while he was working his way through law school.

The attorney general then provided this press release: "Let me tell you what our detectives must put up with in the unfortunate Delorme affair, where leading daily newspapers complete with one another to publish daily sensational accounts. Our detectives cannot pick up a clue, they cannot even come to consult with us at our offices, without having reporters at their heels to report their slightest movements. It is in this manner that the newspapers keep the killers posted on the movements of the detectives and prevent them from working effectively. Not more than two weeks ago I replied in the House to the motion of Mr Sauvé, leader of the opposition, attacking the administration of justice and I showed him that his complaints against the Attorney General's office were without foundation but should have been directed at the press."

On Monday, 13 February, the eve of the inquest, Fernand Roby, a reporter with *La Patrie* whom Father Delorme had befriended, came to tell him he would be arrested next day. Although Father Delorme confidently replied that that was impossible, the same evening a special session of the Provincial Cabinet gave instructions for Delorme's immediate arrest. When Narcisse Arcand told him this next morning, Delorme flew into a rage: "You're crazy. Don't you know this is a cassock? Bibi* has its protection." Menacingly pointing his finger at the reporter and pulling an imaginary trigger, he angrily continued, "Let them try and arrest me! I had a revolver in my car but I have another one here and I won't hesitate, you can be sure." A terrified Arcand hurried out of the Delorme house and headed straight to the police station where he alerted Chief Lepage. The inquest had been set for two o'clock that afternoon but the priest hadn't yet been told of the time. The chief had planned on sending detectives to the Delorme home and have him escorted to the hearing. On hearing Arcand, Lepage changed his mind. Well aware of the priest's unpredictability and sudden bursts of anger, Chief Lepage didn't want to risk a shoot-out. Instead, relying on the good relationship he had developed with the priest, he called him to ask that he come to the station to review new information, as he had done before. Half an hour later Delorme arrived at the police station, where Lepage told him he would keep him in his office for his own security until Coroner McMahon started the inquest at two o'clock.

---

* The expression "Bibi" is commonly used French slang to mean "Me, myself, and I."

Meanwhile, word had spread that the inquest was to reopen. A huge crowd gathered in front of the coroners court, making it almost impossible to deliver the priest. As reported in the February 16th edition of the *New York Times*:

Finding that it was impossible to render the prisoner immune from the gaze of the crowd outside the courthouse exit in any other way, the car was driven up the sidewalk up to the doorway … no happening since the end of the war has caused so much talk as the mystery of Raoul Delorme's death. Father Delorme's queer attitude throughout the investigation and his statements, especially since he learned that suspicion had been directed towards him, have made the case a persistent topic of conversation.

The room in which the inquest was held was filled to the rafters. At two o'clock, when Father Delorme made his entrance, it was so silent you could have heard a pin drop. Delorme approached the bar in a confident and dignified manner. Very much at ease, it appeared that he didn't completely understand how serious his predicament was.

In answer to Walsh's questions, Father Delorme repeated the widely known story of his and Raoul's activities on 6 January, adding only that he had started his car and let the engine idle for a few minutes while working on the furnace. "I might have opened the garage doors and left them that way but I can't say for sure." He also mentioned that Lilly had come down to the basement and chatted with him, as she watched him put the coal in. Was he adding these additional details to make his story consistent with his neighbour's statement at the preceding session? He repeated the story of Raoul's inheritance, adding, "On his death, five years ago, my father appointed me as his only executor as well as Raoul's tutor and administrator. The management of my father's estate was expensive and to help cover the costs I had to borrow from Raoul's inheritance. It was my intention to reimburse him. My brother never complained about it, nor did he ever show that his feelings might have been hurt. Indeed, when he came of age he asked me to continue managing his assets." The priest mentioned that he also managed Florence and Lilly's assets, while Rosa and Claudia managed their own.

As he went on, Father Delorme's tone became rather didactic, with appropriate pauses to allow the court stenographers to properly transcribe what he was saying. Suddenly he appeared to realize that he had not seen his interrogator before. He stopped in mid-sentence, stared at Walsh incredulously as if he were a trespasser, and arro-

gantly asked, "Who are you sir, the coroner?" When Walsh replied
that he had been appointed as special Crown prosecutor, the priest
replied sarcastically, "I understand. Henceforward I will address you
as 'Monsieur l'avocat,' because I insist on addressing everyone by his
title."

Asked why Raoul was still in school at twenty-four years of age, he
answered that he had had to stop for a couple of years because of bad
eyesight. He elaborated on Raoul's character, describing him as an
even-tempered and shy boy who had a rather regular routine: "He
would normally get up around eleven o'clock, play a little piano or
listen to the gramophone, and then go to a movie in the afternoon.
He would often follow that movie with another in the evening."

Walsh questioned him about Raoul's will. Father Delorme
answered that he was in Ottawa when it was signed but, having left
the hospital room when Raoul read it to the two witnesses, he
couldn't testify as to its contents. Walsh called on notary Bélanger
to produce the document but the notary told him he didn't have it
with him and in any event couldn't produce it without the priest's
consent. Irritated by the evasiveness about the will, Walsh ordered
the notary to produce it and Bélanger rushed to his office to get it.
Coroner McMahon shook his head in disbelief and gave the priest
an incredulous look as he called a ten-minute recess. When the
notary returned with the elusive will, it was read to the jury and
produced in the record. Handwritten under the University of Ottawa
letterhead, it stated:

On this 5th day of February, sane of mind and my soul having been recommended to God, I hereby make my will.

I want a first class funeral; I want one thousand masses at $1 each.

I give Florence $1,000 in six years. I give Lilly $1,000 in seven years. I
give Claudia $1,500 in eight years. I give Rosa my brick house at numbers
228 to 296 Amherst St. containing four small lodgings in the yard, possession
of said property to be taken in three years.

I bequeath to my brother my properties on Dorchester and St-Hubert
streets, numbers 177 to 196, including my house at 190 St-Hubert Street and
I also bequeath him my stone house on Amherst Street bearing numbers 278
to 286 as well as all of my clothes, my money, and my debts; my share of
properties in Verdun and my share of any furniture. I bequeath the usufruct
of the money bequeathed to my sisters Florence, Lilly, and Claudia and the
income of the property to my sister Rosa.

I name my brother the "unique" executor of my will.

Signed: Raoul Delorme

Witnesses: Louis Rhéaume O.M.I.
            Docteur Renaud

February 5, 1921.

Questions about the will took up most of the afternoon. Detective Pigeon testified that Father Delorme had given him three different stories about its location. First he had said that it was with notary Bélanger, then that it was in Ottawa, and finally that he didn't know. Chief Lorrain corroborated Pigeon's testimony, adding that the priest had told him, "It's in Ottawa or somewhere, but I couldn't care less. We're rich, we have a lot of money." Lorrain added that Delorme had telephoned him in early February to say that the coroner had lied in stating that the priest had told him he had the will at home. Testimony about Delorme's evasiveness triggered heated exchanges between the priest, Walsh, and some of the witnesses, to the point where Father Delorme suddenly called out to the coroner, "Oh what nonsense!" jumped up from his chair, turned towards the jury, dramatically put his hand on the Bible, stretched out his arms, and shouted "Nothing but the truth" and requested permission to speak, saying "What happened was that a Mr Larivière called me in early February to tell me the coroner mentioned to Chief Lorrain that I had told him I had the will at home. When I told Larivière I didn't, Larivière answered, 'Does the coroner have the right to lie?' I never said I had the will and I never called the coroner a liar, I am too polite for that. I never used that word against anyone."

This sudden interruption occurred in late afternoon. The hearing had been going on for over six hours and everyone was exhausted. The coroner put a stop to any further histrionics by starting his address to the jury. "Gentlemen of the jury, you have a very important duty and you must fulfil it by taking into account only that evidence which has been produced here. Anything you may have heard elsewhere must be put aside. It matters little if Father Delorme said the coroner was a liar. That has no bearing on the case. We have nothing else to do here but our duty. My duty was to give the police all the time they considered necessary to find evidence which could be submitted to you. That has now been done. It is your duty to appreciate and weigh that evidence. You are absolute masters of the facts, judges of the facts. It is up to you to render the verdict. The law obliges the coroner to help you reach a conclusion. The coroner can express his opinion but you are not obliged to follow it. Whatever I may say, be it either for or against anyone, you are free to follow your own conscience when you render judgment, even if your views may differ from mine. On that point you are absolutely independent from anyone. You have heard the proof and I think it unnecessary to summarize it. The first question you must answer is whether or not Raoul Delorme was assassinated. There can be no doubt on that subject. Then you must ask yourselves who killed this young man. In my opinion the evidence put forward today points in one direction. All of the evidence suggests that it is Father Delorme himself who committed the crime."

On hearing this, the priest flinched, turned ashen white, and broke into a nervous smile. He appeared unable to believe that his protective cassock could let him down. A visibly nervous coroner continued, "That is the effect of the evidence. I'm not saying that there isn't any other evidence but none other has been submitted. You must base your verdict on the evidence submitted. Is it sufficient to justify a conclusion that Father Delorme must be arrested and arraigned? It is not your duty to say whether he is guilty, but only if there exists sufficient reasons for him to stand a trial. Two, or I should say three, types of evidence have been put before you. There is the motive for which father Delorme would have killed his half-brother. That would be to benefit from his half-brother's assets. You heard him tell you that the adminstration of his father's estate cost him a lot and that part of the money was taken from his half-brother and his sisters. He said that it was his intention to reimburse the money so borrowed but it is evident that he has not reimbursed anything to date.

Then there's the will. Searches were made to find the will, which father Delorme could have deposited with us immediately. Why such hesitation? Why were we not able to see the contents of the will until the last minute. And now that the will has been produced, we see that it is in favour of the priest with the exception of certain amounts which he will have to pay his sisters but only in several years.

That's the evidence. I am not saying that it is sufficient to find the priest guilty but is it sufficient to have him submit to trial? Is there enough proof to say that there exists a doubt against the priest which justifies his arrest?

Addressing himself to what was unquestionably the most delicate issue before him, he continued, "There is something I feel I have to say. You are all French Canadians and I assume good Roman Catholics. As such, you might naturally hesitate to think a priest could be in such a dubious position. We must, however, perform our duty in the light of the evidence before us. It may be that you have heard Roman Catholics, Protestants, and Freemasons express favourable opinions about Father Delorme. It is also possible that you heard opinions to the contrary. All of that must be put aside. It does not change the evidence. You should not let public opinion or what this or that person thinks affect your decision. Nor should the opinion of the coroner affect you. You must follow your own judgment. You must not be guided by anything you have heard or have read in the newspapers. The newspapers have published many things which have not been proven. And you must not take into account that he is a priest. Your only guide is the evidence that you have heard here. Study it seriously."

The coroner explained that a majority decision was required for a verdict. It was almost six o'clock when he finished his remarks and he excused the jury and wished them well in their deliberations. The jury retired and about an hour later advised the coroner they had reached a verdict. The room was completely silent while an attentive Delorme listened as the jury foreman read the decision:

We, the undersigned jury, after having heard the evidence presented to us, declare that Raoul Delorme died in Montreal on the sixth or seventh of January 1922, killed and murdered in circumstances which permit us to send Father Adélard Delorme before the criminal courts. Clovis Giroux, juryman, dissenting.*

Father Delorme smiled incredulously. He saluted the reporters, waved at the other spectators, asked that the name of the dissenting juryman be repeated, and arrogantly turned on his heels. He was led away under police escort to Chief Lepage's office. He stayed there for several hours while the police chief reported the situation to officials of the Archdiocese of Montreal, assuring them that the prisoner would be treated with all the respect due to his status. Father Delorme interjected that he was happy to have been arrested because it would finally clarify things. "I'm not afraid of being tried," he said, "because no man alive will find me guilty on the basis of such weak evidence." He was then taken to a holding cell for the night. On entering he took a look around and remarked, "This is a nice place."

---

* The verdict was signed by Edgar Mercier, Charles Eugène Thibault, Albany Payette, Edgar Perreault, Georges Leduc, and Louis Paré.

The next morning a black limousine headed north with Father Delorme, Chiefs Lepage and Lorrain, and three of their assistants. During his long ride the priest read reports of the verdict in the morning newspaper. A special edition had been published and within hours the whole country had learned of the verdict. The international press described the story as "the most important criminal case in Canadian history." A front-page headline story in the 15 February edition of the *New York Times* reported "Priest Is Accused of Killing Brother to Get Insurance." It seemed incredible that a Roman Catholic priest could be tried for murder in the devoutly Catholic City of Steeples, a city which Mark Twain had once labelled as the only city he had been in "where one could not throw a brickbat without breaking a church window." In the limousine, the mood was relaxed. "What this case tells us" said the priest, "is that we should keep our mouths shut." There was a lot of casual small talk as they rode. In fact, the atmosphere was so congenial that at one point Father Delorme asked Chief Lorrain if he would get him a supply of mint candies. Lorrain had the driver stop, ran to a nearby store and returned with two full bags. Delorme passed them around and continued to chat as the limousine made its way to Bordeaux prison.

A terrifying facility, Bordeaux Prison had been built in 1913 on twenty acres of land near Rivière des Prairies on the north edge of the island of Montreal. Its 1,200 cells, built in six three-storey wings that jutted out like spider legs from a large hub, housed every type of criminal from petty thieves to the murderers who were hanged on one of the two scaffolds that stood on the outside of the hub between two of the wings.*

On arriving, as Father Delorme was ushered to the receiving office and turned over to the prison officials, Chief Lorrain gave him a warm handshake, "Well Father, here we are, *au revoir* and good luck." The priest looked at the police chiefs who had been so much a part of his life for the past few weeks and burst into tears. He quickly composed himself, replied, "*Au revoir*, Gentlemen; thank you," and blessed them with the traditional hand gesture as he watched them walk away.

At about the same time that Father Delorme entered his cell, Farah-Lajoie knocked on the door at 190 St-Hubert Street. It had been a month since his last visit. He was delighted to have achieved his objective of having Delorme arrested. He could now continue his investigation without having to put up with the presence of Father

---

* Eighty-three murderers met their fate on those scaffolds. The last execution was in 1960.

Delorme and his influence on potential witnesses. He was greeted with bitterness by the priest's sisters. Despite their open resentment – among other things, they accused him of having stolen their brother's coat for his personal use – he searched the house again and found quilts in Florence's room which perfectly matched those found around Raoul's head. He had no doubt they had been made by the same person. Over the sisters' protests, he took the quilts to the police station.

Although Delorme's absence gave Farah-Lajoie more freedom in his investigation, he had underestimated the solidarity of Montreal's Catholic community. While the Archbishop had asked priests to remain neutral, it appeared that there was a coordinated effort to make things as difficult as possible for the detective. Morning prayers at his children's schools now included pleas for divine help to save his soul. His wife, a devout Roman Catholic, did not entirely agree with his persistence in his investigation. Knowing this, her parish priest seized every opportunity to have her exert her influence. "He could be innocent, Georges" she said. "Don't you think you should look for other suspects?" she asked him as delicately as possible. He replied abruptly, "Marie Anne, that man murdered his brother. Don't interfere with my work." For the sake of family harmony, they agreed that the Delorme case was not to be a topic of conversation in their home. This didn't, however, reduce outside pressures. In addition to being shunned at school, some of his children were subjected to physical and oral abuse. There was even a plot to burn down the Farah-Lajoie home. At one point Monsignor Paul Bruchési, the influential archbishop of Montreal, got in touch with Farah-Lajoie. He told him that although he couldn't order him to stop doing his job, he would appreciate it if the detective were not quite so zealous. Farah-Lajoie replied, "When you and I started our occupations we each took an oath to be faithful to our duties. I consider the value of my oath to be the same as yours." The detective received many anonymous letters accusing him of being an anti-clerical or a pagan bribed by Freemasons and other secret societies to have the priest condemned. A weekly newspaper, *l'Autorité*, published a story that he had received $25,000 from Freemasons to pursue the case and would receive another $25,000 if he could send Father Delorme to the gallows. Many of Farah-Lajoie's colleagues, superiors, friends, and neighbours began to keep away from him, as if he had the plague. However, his reputation for integrity, his mental and physical stamina, and support from the attorney general's office and from his chief allowed him to withstand this and continue his investigation.

The Coroner's jury had determined that Father Delorme should be brought before the courts. A preliminary hearing would now be held to decide if there was sufficient evidence to commit him to trial.*

Gustave and Philippe Monette had been retained to defend Delorme. Gustave Monette, thirty-five years old and a graduate of College Ste-Thérèse, Father Delorme's own Alma Mater, was already a highly respected lawyer. A tall, slim man with aquiline features and a somewhat aristocratic bearing, his deep voice made him an outstanding pleader and a most persuasive orator. Philippe Monette, his cousin, was an expert in criminal law and was soon to form the first firm in Montreal to devote itself exclusively to that specialty.

The preliminary hearing was held on Tuesday, 21 February. A crowd of several hundred had gathered around the prisoners' entrance to the court house where the prison van made its daily delivery of prisoners. In order to discourage demonstrations and because threats had been made against both the priest and the police, a decoy was arranged. Father Delorme arrived secretly at the front door in an unmarked private car as the prison van arrived at its usual side entrance. He was rushed to the judge's chambers where Judge Victor Cusson quickly postponed the start of the hearing until 7 March at the request of Delorme's lawyers. Meanwhile the prison van was discharging several prison officials and the decoy, a prison guard dressed in a dark coat with upturned collar and a black fedora resembling Delorme's. The thick cordon of policemen around him made it difficult to get a close look. By the time the onlookers and press reporters realized what had happened, Delorme was on his way back to Bordeaux in the unmarked car, having greatly enjoyed being the central figure of such intrigue.

This postponement, and the one which followed, angered Farah-Lajoie. Having devoted much time and effort to getting the investigation this far, he didn't want to see the system defeat him. To avoid the risk of bureaucratic bungling and delays he had personally written out the subpoenas for twenty-seven witnesses.

When the hearing finally opened on 14 March, Gustave Monette took the floor and made a surprising statement: he claimed that Father Delorme was mentally unstable and requested a further postponement until a medical examination could establish whether his

---

* A hearing by a judge prior to indictment during which the Crown is required to produce sufficient evidence to establish that there is probable cause to believe (a) that a crime has been committed and (b) that the defendant committed it.

client was fit to stand trial. He pointed out that Delorme's eccentricities and unusual behaviour were well-known and more than justified his request. Judge Cusson rejected the request. He said that it was premature and told the lawyers to proceed.

Nothing new was revealed during the early part of the hearing. Several witnesses established when and how the body was found, the cause of death, and the activities in and around the Delorme house on the night of 6 January. Farah-Lajoie quickly reviewed all the evidence he had found, including the discovery that the bullets found in Raoul's body matched those fired from the priest's Bayard; the twenty-eight bullets found in the bullet boxes, which had originally contained fifty, left fourteen bullets unaccounted for after the eight fired in Hayne's target range when the gun was purchased were subtracted; the quilts around Raoul's body matched those found in the Delorme home; the feather found in the priest's car matched a feather found on the quilt around Raoul's body; the blood found on the cushion in the priest's car had been found to be human; the rope in the Delorme basement matched the one which held the quilt around Raoul's head; the soap stains on the seat of Delorme's car matched those on the quilts; and two pairs of Raoul's overshoes were found at his home but there were none on his feet when his body was discovered.

The boredom resulting from the repetitious evidence quickly ended near the finish of the afternoon session when Chief Lorrain revealed that on 4 February a Pall Mall box had been delivered to his home containing Delorme's gold watch. The paper wrapper gave Lorrain's home address and the inscription, "A. Delorme watch." The watch was attached to a broken chain, which suggested it had been ripped off Raoul's vest. But what had happened to the other piece of chain, which would normally have been found dangling from Raoul's vest? Why had it been removed? On hearing this, Farah-Lajoie remembered how often he had thrown his empty Pall Mall box into Father Delorme's waste basket as he chatted with him in his study. It was also commonly known that the detective smoked that brand. Had the priest taken the watch from Raoul's body and tried to discredit Farah-Lajoie by sending it to the police in a box which could be easily identified with him, perhaps hoping people would think he had stolen it when he checked on Raoul's personal effects at the morgue?

Next morning the audience was in for another surprise. A headless tailor's mannequin dressed in the bloodstained clothes found on Raoul's body was wheeled into the courtroom. This sort of display was unusual in a Montreal courtroom and reactions ranged from amusement to horror. The idea of the dummy had been Farah-Lajoie's. It was a prop for Dr Wilfrid Derome, who was called as the first witness.

Derome testified that the blood and car grease on the cap and the quilt matched that found on the cushion and blankets from the back seat of Delorme's car. With the help of the mannequin he described how Raoul had been shot. Six bullets had been fired into him. He showed how the bullet hole in the shirt collar, the path of the bullets, and the pattern of the bloodstains on Raoul's shirt and underwear established that the shooting had taken place at close range while Raoul was leaning over. Since the coat found on Raoul's body did not have any corresponding bullet holes, Derome concluded that the murder had taken place indoors, and that the coat had later been put on the dead body. A handwritten statement Father Delorme had given a reporter was then produced and Derome went on to establish scientifically that it was the same handwriting as that which appeared on the Pall Mall box used to mail the watch to Chief Lorrain. Although Derome was rigorously cross-examined by Gustave Monette, his testimony remained firm.

Another startling revelation was made when Father Louis Rhéaume OMI, rector of the University of Ottawa, testified that Father Delorme had helped Raoul write his will in his Ottawa hospital room shortly before his appendectomy in early 1921. Rhéaume explained that as rector of the university it was his custom to visit hospitalized students. When he arrived at the hospital about forty-five minutes before Raoul's operation, he found Raoul and Adélard working on the will. It was then signed in the hospital room in the presence of Rhéaume and a doctor, who acted as witnesses.

Rhéaume was followed to the stand by notary Bélanger, with whom the will had been deposited. He testified that a few days after Raoul's death the priest had called him, asking that he unseal the will and summarize its contents to him over the telephone. When Bélanger showed a certain hesitation, the priest angrily insisted "Read it to me over the phone. I want to know if any Masses are to be sung and who the executor is."

Théophile Marot, an actuary with La Sauvegarde Assurance Company, then told the court that the initiative for the insurance on Raoul's life had been taken by Father Delorme, who had showed up unannounced at the company's offices on 19 December 1921, saying that he had a $25,000 risk to insure. He remembered the priest specifically asking that the policy be made payable to Raoul's estate in order to facilitate loans against it as well as to ease the administration of his will. Marot stated that Father Delorme had told him he knew the will's contents.

Throughout the two days of the hearing, Father Delorme listened impassively to the testimony, nonchalantly sucking on his mint candies while taking lengthy notes. He occasionally smiled at the prison officials sitting next to him and made a point of waving at various press reporters he recognized in the audience.

His relaxed behaviour changed to one of concern when the evidence was complete and Judge Cusson said he was ready to hand down his decision. Concern became worried indignation when he heard the judge state, "There has been no witness to a murder but there has undeniably been one and the facts revealed at this preliminary inquiry are sufficient to authorize me to say that the accused must stand trial, must defend himself." Once again Father Delorme was led away to the cells.

The decision was not unanimously popular, to say the least. Letters poured into Gustave Monette's office supporting the priest. As expected, some maintained he was being framed. Others accused Farah-Lajoie of being involved in a personal vendetta and of abusing his authority. Accusations were also made about the sisters' boy friends and about Leclerc. Rumours that Rosa's boyfriend, Richard Davis, was black had made him a convenient target. A group of spiritualists published a notice in the newspapers and distributed a pamphlet around Montreal.

MESSAGE FROM BEYOND

During a séance of very serious spiritualists, without having been invoked and to everyone's great surprise, the spirit of Raoul Delorme appeared to declare his brother innocent of the crime of which he was being accused. He dictated the following affidavit:

"I, the undersigned Raoul Delorme affirm having accidentally shot myself while trying to kill my fellow man. As I shot, the weapon turned on me and I went down. The cause of it all was mutual love. My brother is innocent. If you condemn him you will be condemning an innocent man and God will judge you accordingly.

[signed] Raoul Delorme

Delorme is innocent. If you condemn him, you will be condemning an innocent man. Courage my brother. I am watching over you. No one can condemn you. I come from beyond to save you, if Justice lives by its real name 'Justice.'

Yours from the heart

Raoul Delorme"

Back in Bordeaux Prison, Father Delorme asked to see its governor, the Honourable Napoléon Séguin. Séguin testified that on entering the governor's office, Delorme told him he was hungry and would like to eat. Séguin politely reminded Delorme that he was not in prison to give orders. Father Delorme quickly changed his tactic, complained of being very hungry, and softly pleaded, "Please understand that I must eat to remain healthy. Would you be kind enough to have dinner prepared for me?" The governor was touched. He invited Father Delorme to join him and ordered that two meals be brought to his office. From that point a special relationship developed between the governor and his star prisoner. Séguin visited Father Delorme on a daily basis and also personally drove him to and from the courthouse each day instead of putting him in the prison van with the other prisoners.

Prison did not seem to bother Father Delorme. He slept about twelve hours a night and his healthy appetite grew to gargantuan proportions: his daily breakfast included a pound of steak. When not eating or sleeping, he spent hours writing to influential figures such as Médéric Martin, the mayor of Montreal, and Sir Lomer Gouin, minister of justice, urging them to help him or inviting them to visit. He also sent several daily notes to the governor asking that he make telephone calls on his behalf for a variety of purposes ranging from the preparation of his defence to the management of his properties. But despite all the conveniences he enjoyed, it was apparent that he had lost all authority. The Church had even suspended his right to say Mass and administer the Holy Sacraments, pending the result of his trial. How well his ego would accept these changes remained to be seen.

A Question of Sanity

The 1922 summer term of the King's Bench opened on Thursday, 1 June, with the Honourable Dominique Monet presiding.* A stern man who didn't take fools lightly, Monet was highly respected for his integrity and solid judicial thinking. At the age of twenty-six he had been elected to the House of Commons as member from Napierville in his friend Sir Wilfrid Laurier's government, where he had made his mark as a brilliant orator. Never reluctant to fight openly for his beliefs, no matter how controversial, he resigned from the House of Commons in 1899 in protest against Canada's participation in the Boer war. He was later elected to the provincial legislature, where he served as cabinet minister. He once travelled to Rome to personally plead with the pope against the decision of the archbishops of St Hyacinthe and Montreal to refuse to relocate a seminary to Monet's home town of St Jean. That challenge to the local clerical authority helped label him as anticlerical – despite his being a devout Catholic.

The drama was to unfold in the Palais de Justice – the Old Courthouse, as it came to be known to the public. A stately grey stone building designed along classic lines, it was reached by climbing huge steps which led through a row of tall Ionic pillars. Built in the mid-1800s, it took up almost an entire city block at "Dead Man's Curve," the label given the narrow junction of Notre-Dame and St James streets in the heart of the legal and financial districts. At its rear was the immense Champ de Mars military parade ground, the site of many demonstrations over the years, the latest of which had been the

---

* Dominique Monet was a cousin of both Gustave Monette and Philippe Monette, the defendant's lawyers. (See footnote, p. xi.)

anticonscription riots during World War I. Inside, the Old Court-house's most impressive features were the beautiful woodwork and wrought iron that could be seen everywhere, from the impressive railings of the large central stairway, to the judges' dais and the prisoners dock in the high ceilinged courtrooms, to the quaint metal elevators noisily rattling up and down in their latticed iron cages.

As usual, the trial began with the reading of the court roll. When the clerk reached the name of Adélard Delorme, Judge Monet broke his habit of not giving the jury panel preliminary instructions. He felt justified in this change because of the controversial pre-trial pub-licity and the unique circumstances of presiding over a trial in which a jury of Roman Catholics would have to decide if a priest went to the gallows. He pointed out that the accused was being referred to as Delorme, "because we are no longer concerned with Father Delorme, but with Delorme pure and simple. The religious authorities have deprived him of the character of priesthood in depriving him of his cassock. I know most of you are good Catholics but you cannot, for a moment, think of the cassock he once wore. Please consider him simply as a layman who has never been a reverend." Delorme was then led into the prisoner's dock. The Clerk read the indictment.

You are accused under the name of Adélard Delorme of having, during the night of January sixth to January seventh last, committed the crime of murder upon Raoul Delorme. What do you say? Are you guilty or not guilty of the charge as drawn against you?

Delorme didn't answer. The courtroom was totally silent for more than thirty seconds waiting for a reply. As the accused made a move to sit down, Judge Monet curtly called out to the clerk, "Tell the prisoner to remain standing." Delorme did so, but still didn't answer the charge. Finally his lawyer stated that the defence intended to submit a preliminary plea of insanity* because Delorme was not

---

* This plea should not be confused with the insanity plea which seeks to have the accused acquitted because he was insane when he committed the crime and therefore didn't know what he was doing. The preliminary plea of insanity is founded on the rule that someone accused of a crime must be able to understand the charge against him to properly defend himself. It seeks to postpone the trial until the accused is declared fit. It focuses on his mental condition at the time of the trial, not the crime. A recent example (April 1994) is the Matchee case in which Master Cpl Clayton Matchee was considered too severely brain damaged (as a result of a suicide attempt) to stand trial for the torture and murder of a Somali teenager during a UN famine-relief mission.

mentally fit to present an intelligent defence and was therefore unfit for trial. Under the circumstances, he had advised the accused not to answer the charge.

After a brief discussion with the lawyers, the judge fixed 9 June as the trial date and left the room without further comment. Delorme was led away to the cells. The preliminary plea of insanity was a rarely used procedure, unfamiliar to the general public. The audience in the courtroom was stunned. Everyone had come to see a show, but there were no actors. Did this plea mean Delorme would be freed? Would there be another trial? What was going on? The spectators left the Court House looking at each other quizzically.

On Saturday, 3 June, the *Montreal Herald* published a sensational story. Claiming that Delorme had told Farah-Lajoie as early as 9 January that he had killed his brother at his home on 6 January between four o'clock and ten o'clock, rendering him unconscious by attacking from behind with an ether-doused handkerchief and then shooting him in the head. The priest had even assured himself that Raoul had taken the Holy Sacraments of Penance and Communion earlier in the day. The article also claimed that the attorney general's office had been advised of Delorme's confession. Within twenty-four hours the story spread to newspapers throughout the world. Farah-Lajoie categorically denied the story and demanded a retraction, "It is obvious that this case has aroused public opinion. As to my character, it has already been attacked by both the press and anonymous letters; by rumour-mongers who are as unfair as they are uninformed. I know of all the insults and invectives directed at me. I have been falsely labelled a freemason, an atheist, a freethinker, an anti-clerical, an anarchist, etc. I have even been accused of having been handsomely paid by heretics and infidels to have a priest convicted of murder. Throughout all this, I remained silent. I am breaking my silence today because now I have been denounced in public." The attorney general's office also denied the story.

Judge Monet felt he had to do something. A couple of days after the story in the *Herald*, he issued a public statement that newspapers should be very prudent when reporting on the case. The *Herald* story, he said, "can create public prejudice against either Delorme or the Crown because it goes beyond exposing the facts: it makes sensational statements that can hinder the case. I will not repeat its content," he continued, "because this would be too dangerous. However, I ask those who have not yet read it not to do so and those who have, to disregard it. The detective about whom accusations are made is

extremely honest and his integrity is known by all who know him. I
therefore ask all newspapers to be extremely cautious in a case where
the freedom, and the life, of a man is at stake."

In the meantime Judge Monet's instructions to the jury came under
fire from certain members of the clergy. On 6 June Father E.T.
Lachapelle, chaplain of Bordeaux Prison, sent him this letter under
the letterhead of the parish of St Joseph de Bordeaux:

To his honour Judge D. Monette

Your Honour,

The newspapers quote you as making an error in religious doctrine which I
believe you should rectify, because it would be unfortunate if our people came
to believe that a judge is ignorant of his catechism to that extent.

You have been quoted as saying that in depriving Father Delorme of his
cassock the religious authorities deprived him of the character of priesthood.
It should not be forgotten that the cassock does not imprint any character in
the soul of a Christian. It is the Sacrament of Ordination conferred by the
Bishop which imprints this character. Even the Pope is incapable of removing
it and far less so a Judge.

Thus Father Delorme remains Father Delorme, despite your insistence on
calling him Adélard.

The character of priesthood is always worthy of respect by real Christians,
even if the person bearing it is a renegade. Our Lord and His Holy Mother
respected Judas, despite his treason. Father Delorme is, after all, simply a
person accused of murder. I have no objection, your Honour, to your giving
my letter to the newspapers.

Yours truly in J.C.

E.T. Lachapelle, Parish priest, Chaplain of the Montreal Prison.

Although the largest of the courtrooms, Room 12 was filled to the
breaking point on Friday, 9 June. A predominantly female audience,
described by one newspaper as "unusually elegant for the court-
house," filled it. It was a very chic gathering indeed. Many of the
ladies wore the latest, and rather startling, loose-fitting two-piece
suits created by an innovative young French designer named Coco
Chanel. The array of hats was equally impressive. The courtroom
resembled the premiere of an opera with "le tout Montréal" present.

All eyes focused on the prisoner's dock as a pale and tired-looking Delorme made his entrance.

Undoubtedly on the advice of his lawyers, who would not allow the jury to forget he was a priest, he wore a black clerical suit and roman collar. As an added touch, a black-bordered white handkerchief projected from his lapel pocket, a sign of mourning for his dead brother. The audience let out a sigh of disappointment when the Crown requested a postponement, stating that one of its expert medical witnesses had just arrived in town and needed time to examine Delorme and prepare his testimony. An astonished judge adjourned in order to confer with the lawyers in his chambers. He returned shortly and set 15 June as the new date, insisting that no more postponements would be tolerated.

Judge Monet's displeasure with the press because of the *Herald's* story of 3 June turned to indignation when the 12 June edition of *La Presse* reported that a team of mental specialists had examined the priest and unanimously declared him insane and unfit for trial. This was too much for the judge. He refused to tolerate the press taking over the role of the judiciary. He got in touch with *La Presse* and ordered a retraction and the publication of a statement he drafted, clearly explaining the judicial process involved in the insanity plea. It was delivered to the newspaper's office with a note advising that refusal to print it would mean exclusion of *La Presse* from his courtroom. The statement appeared in the next day's edition.

We erred yesterday in declaring that the five mental specialists in the Delorme case had rendered a unanimous verdict declaring that the accused suffered from amorality and intellectual debility which would justify his internment without a trial.

The truth is that the mental specialists do not have the right to give a verdict in this matter. All they have a right to do is for each of them to render his testimony under oath before the jury and the judge. The jury alone, not even the judge, has the right to render a verdict declaring that the accused is not sane or is in a state to stand his trial. It can do this only after having heard the evidence given by the mental specialists. The accused, having been indicted, is obliged to appear before the petit jury and we have erred in saying that the file as to his mental health or state is considerable enough for Adélard Delorme to be interned without any testimony and that he need not submit to any trial before the Assizes. The truth is that the expert witnesses will have to be heard and that the jury will have to declare, by their verdict, not whether or not the accused is guilty, but whether or not he is sane enough to stand trial."

Judge Monet was determined not to allow the media to take control of the trial over which it was his duty to preside. Although it was unusual for a judge to make public statements in such circumstances, characteristically, he chose to fight any publicity-seeking intervention and hoped the published statement would put an end to the confusion introduced by an irresponsible press. A story in the 14 June edition of the *New York Times* quoted him as saying that the conclusion about the mental specialists was a "veritable lie."

The hearing finally got under way on 15 June, in the midst of a heat wave. Although Delorme appeared edgy as he was escorted into the prisoner's dock, he soon calmed down and seemed rather amused at the procedure of selecting and rejecting members of the jury. He chuckled each time a prospective juror was excused and walked back to his seat.

After a tedious and time-consuming selection, the jury was set* and Crown Prosecutor Walsh took the floor. He outlined the issue before them in his opening remarks, making it clear that the jury's duty was not to decide if the accused had murdered his brother but whether or not he was fit to be tried for that crime. Did his mental faculties permit him to understand what was going on around him? If they did, he was fit to be tried. If not, he would be confined to a mental institution until such time as the lieutenant governor of the province considered him ready for trial. Finally, he explained that in this particular preliminary plea the burden of proof was on the defence and not on the Crown as was usually the case. So the defence would be the first to present its case.

As its first witnesses, the defence called officials of l'Hôpital St Jean de Dieu. They produced hospital records showing that a number of Delorme's relatives had experienced mental problems. Adélard's mother, Eugénie Grenier, had been admitted to the institution in 1891 and died a few months later. His aunt had been a patient in the same institution for eight years. His maternal grandfather and two uncles had also been admitted there but for shorter periods. On his father's side, a great uncle, an uncle, an aunt, and a cousin had suffered

---

* The members of the jury were Herméningilde Godin, Napoléon Tison, Louis E. Robin, A. Loriot, Côme Lapierre, Joseph L'Archevêque, Hubert Robert, Wilfrid Desjardins, Adélard Goulet, Amédée Thibault, Joseph Gagnon, and Napoléon Lamarre. In Quebec, women were ineligible for jury duty until 1971.

Delorme family tree

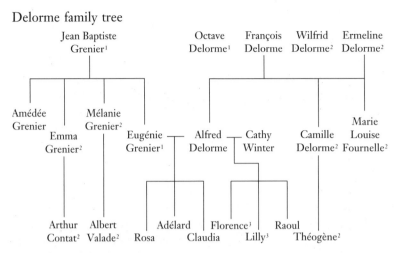

[1] died of mental disease
[2] suffered from mental disease requiring hospitalizaton
[3] retarded

different degrees of insanity and had also been hospitalized. One of them, Marie-Louise Fournel, was described as a notorious imbecile. Including Lilly and Florence, who were generally considered to be retarded, no fewer than fourteen members of Adélard's family had suffered from some type of mental disorder. The jury heard additional testimony about senility, birth disorders, and alcoholism in both families.

Angéline Delorme, the accused's aunt, testified that the accused had been very ill at the age of two and that there might have been residual effects from that illness.

The defence's case for insanity was greatly helped by the testimonies of Florence and Lilly. Both were unsure of how long they had been in school, and Florence was unable to remember her date of birth. Monette tested Florence's knowledge:

"So you learned mathematics and religious history, did you?"

"Yes."

"If I sent you to the grocery store with $1 and you bought a dozen apples for $0.29, how much change would you get?"

"I wasn't very good in maths, you know."

"I suppose you were better in religious history."

"Yes."

"Sem, Cham and Japhet were Noah's three sons. What was their father's name?"

"I don't remember, Sir."

A titter ran back and forth across the courtroom, but was quickly subdued by a stern look from the judge.

Lilly's testimony was no better. When Monette asked her if she could count backwards from twenty she answered affirmatively and confidently called out "19, 17, 18, 16, 11, 10, 7, 8, 4, 3, 2, 1." She failed to give the proper answer to other simple questions on mathematics and religion. Finally she broke into tears, saying, "I had to quit school because of poor eyesight. If I had continued I would have gone blind."

Both girls had been very reluctant during their testimony and kept directing embarrassed glances at the accused, looking for support. They had each come to court impeccably dressed in dark skirts and the latest ruffle-collared white blouses. Humbly sitting in the witness box, wearing cloche hats carefully adjusted over their neatly cut hair, they had wanted to make a good impression for their brother and couldn't appreciate the irony that their failure to answer correctly had actually helped his cause.

The court was next given a glimpse of Delorme's behaviour behind bars. Napoleon Séguin, governor of Bordeaux Prison, said he was in constant touch with the accused and never saw him show any signs of emotion. Even Raoul's death, which he often discussed with the prisoner, drew no emotional reaction from him. There were no signs of tenderness or sadness. Delorme would simply ask, "What reason would I have had to kill my brother? We lived happily together." As to his sisters' visits, he commented that the first time a prisoner was visited from close relatives he inevitably broke into tears. However, when Séguin ushered Rosa, Lilly, and Florence into the accused's cell, "they simply shook hands, smiled, and asked each other how they were. And they hugged one another. I allowed them to hug. It was like a family visit on New Year's day, noisy and gay. He gave them a tour of his cell, jokingly saying he was on a closed retreat." Séguin and other officials were always surprised at Delorme's constant good humour during the preliminary hearing. "We never heard him sound nervous. His appetite remained good. And although the rest of us were sometimes shaken by some of the testimony we heard, it never seemed to bother him." Séguin said the only time he saw Delorme show any emotion was when he had reproached him for trying to send letters without going through channels. "I reprimanded him and told him that if he tried that again, I would have to punish him. At that point, Delorme closed his eyes, curled his lower lip like a scolded child, looked up at me and said, 'I forgot. Anyway, I didn't do it maliciously.'"

The prison doctor, Dr Emmanuel Benoît, testified that he didn't find Delorme to be in a normal mental state. "Some of his mannerisms led me to believe he was insane." Benoît singled out Delorme's failure to appreciate his predicament, his constant belief that he would be freed momentarily, his conviction that everyone was working toward that end, and his total preoccupation with himself. The witness thought Delorme was a megalomaniac. The judge asked if the accused's obsession with himself meant he was not sane enough to be tried, which, he reminded the witness, was the only point at issue. "Is he able to conduct a reasonable defence?" he asked. Benoît answered that he was convinced Delorme could not.

The prison chaplain, Father Eugène Lachapelle, then testified. He concentrated on the accused's vanity, noting how happy he was about his newly acquired fame. "The accused seemed concerned more with how he looked in court than with anything else. He rambled on in his cell about how he would confuse his adversaries during the trial, how he would make a five-hour opening statement and would end his trial with an eight-hour plea."

The defence then unexpectedly called Dr Wilfrid Derome, the forensic surgeon. As head of the Montreal Crime Laboratory, Derome was an official of the Crown. Nevertheless, Gustave Monette was confident he would be helpful to his cause. Derome proceeded to corroborate much of what Benoît had said. Since early January, he had seen Delorme approximately ten times, the first time when he identified his brother's body at the morgue. He, too, was struck by his verbosity, vanity, and sense of exaggerated worth. He had visions of grandeur which went beyond the absurd. As an example, Derome referred to the priest's request that the killer be hanged in the Mount Royal Arena. He mentioned Delorme's habit of referring to himself braggingly as "*Bibi*" and of ordering people around. He also spoke of his first meeting with Delorme at the morgue. "His brother's body was lying on the floor when he was ushered into the morgue to identify it the day after the murder. I had never seen him before and was told he was the victim's brother. I couldn't help but observe him. He acted as if it were a stranger's body. He didn't show the slightest sign of emotion or affection. Nothing – absolute indifference. That was the first thing that struck me. I was amazed with a similar lack of emotion during all our visits with him throughout the investigation, before he was accused of the murder."

He also thought that Delorme had tried to be evasive. He said Delorme was self-assured and believed he would come out of the trial in good shape. He was sure his wealth and status would provide him with the means to overcome anything. Derome said it was some of those self-assured statements that had attracted police suspicion. The witness felt that on balance the accused was not fit to stand trial and stressed the evidence about his heredity, claiming that it was the strongest he had ever seen.

As Dr Derome went on about the intellectual weakness of the Delorme sisters, Judge Monet got the uncomfortable impression that the Crown wasn't putting forth its best effort. Walsh wasn't cross-examining with his usual aggressiveness and the witness was too quick to say that Delorme was mentally incompetent. That bothered Judge Monet, especially since Derome was a Crown official. His testimony was so favourable to the defence's position that even Delorme's own lawyer remarked on it: "You haven't been asked to find something helpful to the defence?" "Oh, not at all," came the answer.

Judge Monet didn't like what he was hearing. The earlier press reports had been bad enough, but any apparent special treatment of the accused by the Crown would be totally unacceptable in his courtroom. He would not risk such a mockery of the law. So once again, he characteristically jumped into the fray. If Walsh wasn't going to ask the right question, he would. As a general rule, judges did not get directly involved in the questioning of a witness. They sometimes sought clarification of an answer, but went no further. Such would not be the case here. He interrupted Derome and asked about Rosa. The witness began hedging, saying he preferred not giving details because he was not a specialist in mental disease and had never examined the accused or his sisters. Following further questioning by the judge, he admitted that an intelligent person in the accused's situation could fake insanity and that his letters to the Quebec premier, the minister of justice, and the mayor did not show any degree of insanity. "But," replied Derome, "the reasons he invoked and his request that they use their influence are not the mark of a serious man. They show a lack of perception." The judge read certain flattering passages which the accused had underlined in his letter to the premier and asked, "Isn't that a sign of shrewd-ness and logic, considering that the letters were written to politicians who thrive on that kind of thing?" The witness, however, persisted and said he considered it abnormal for a thirty-five-year-old college graduate to think that the minister of justice would exempt him from due process of law. It showed a lack of judgment and moral sense. The judge reminded Derome that history was full of crooked politicians without any moral sense. "They might be judged to have been dishonest," he said, "but it doesn't follow that they were insane."

Derome replied that isolated instances in a person's life could not be used to determine insanity. Continuity was important. "One can't rely on accidental behaviour," he said. The judge replied, "So, according to you, a politician who had been dishonest seven, eight, nine, or ten times instead of only once would have a good chance of being considered incompetent to be tried?" Somewhat hesitatingly Derome replied, "Well, those are special cases. Some politicians would be so considered. But to quote a number ... six, seven, eight ... I would say it's the repetition. That's the point I want to emphasize the repetition." Judge Monet then sarcastically asked, "Could you tell us at about what number sanity stops?" "No I can't" replied Derome.

The judge ended his questions on that note. It was apparent that he didn't believe Delorme was criminally insane. To the great relief of everyone, he adjourned until the next morning. The humid heat wave that had been hanging over the city for several days had made the crowded courtroom unbearably stuffy, so much so that a juryman had fainted and the proceeding had had to be interrupted for two hours. This had prompted the judge to adjourn for fifteen minutes every hour and clear the courtroom. It might have also taken its toll on the judge who, throughout the trial, finished off his exhausting days in court by spending sleepless nights at home going through his mountain of mail and pouring over medical research on mental disease.

Next day's proceedings began with the testimony of Dr Joseph Handfield. He had known Delorme for seventeen years and owned rental property near the Delorme house. For over four years he had seen Delorme on a regular basis at the neighbourhood service station and said the priest acted extravagantly and loved to attract an audience. "He would talk and gesticulate at great length about his automobile trips and his wealth, giving the impression he was worth millions. So many words would pour out of his mouth that I thought he was in a state of frenzied self-glorification. He was the neighbourhood clown. He would take any flattering remark seriously, not realizing that his audience was amusing itself at his expense. He bragged about how much rent he was collecting from his properties and even about how much money he would make with his trial. I could have signed an order for his internment on the spot and I don't believe it would have been refused. When I asked him why he didn't exercise his ministry, he said the archdiocese wanted him to but he told them he was too busy managing his business affairs and that they had no choice but to listen to him."

Handfield told the court about a bizarre incident. "On the eve of Delorme's arrest, I happened to see him on the street. I hadn't seen him since his brother's death so I extended my condolences. Instead of giving the usual response, he started shouting and gesticulating. 'You'll see what I'll do to those newspapers. I'll sue them. I'll make two million dollars with this thing.' That's when I decided he was a maniac." The witness then described the priest's reaction when he offered to replace Raoul as his travelling companion. "Perfect," he replied, but seemed anxious to return to his favourite topic. "You'll see, I'll get a lot of money. I'll live well with the money I'll get from this thing." Judge Monet interrupted: "I'm sure you know the adage 'an ass and an ass make two asses and the two make a pair.' Could you explain, doctor, why, over four-and-a-half years you chatted with the accused for hours on end?" Handfield replied that there had been no real camaraderie with the accused. The judge then asked him why, if that was the case, he had offered to replace Raoul as the priest's travelling companion. When Handfield replied that he had been joking, Monet asked, "You are an intelligent man, a doctor. What kind of pleasure can you get out of mocking a fool?"

It was now 3:45 on Friday, 16 June, and there had been no relief from the heat. When the Crown requested an adjournment, Judge Monet granted it. He welcomed the break because for the last few days he had been fighting a persistent flu. In a somewhat paternalistic tone he suggested that the sheriff organize a variety of outdoor activities for the jury: "A lot of fresh air and walks on Mount-Royal will do them a world of good." Delorme chatted with his sisters for a few minutes and, according to the June 17 *Toronto Globe*, was overheard saying he was "impressed at being famous in a fine trial." As usual, he left for Bordeaux in the prison governor's unmarked car.

When the trial resumed on Monday morning, Handfield continued his testimony, stating that Delorme had the mentality of a seven-year-old. He suggested he had been renting Raoul's properties out as bordellos and was involved in bootlegging. The defence was obviously attempting to persuade the jury by stressing Delorme's amorality, unusual behaviour, and lack of sensibility. The judge, however, felt that Handfield was a pompous bigot who liked to pontificate about morality and who was perhaps jealous of the accused's wealth.

Fernand Roby, the reporter from *La Patrie* was then called to the stand. He had followed the case from the start and kept in close contact with Delorme. He told the court how, when he first called at the St Hubert Street house the day after the discovery of the body, "I was greeted by a courteous and good-humoured Delorme who showed me around the house, pointing out how richly furnished it was, much in the way of a museum guide." Roby said he had been somewhat puzzled by this, considering that the priest had just learned of the murder of his brother. He had spoken with the priest on a daily basis after that. He told how, while visiting Delorme, one of his tenants had arrived to negotiate an adjustment in his rent. "Father Delorme escorted the tenant into his office and emerged several times during his meeting to have me check his pulse, saying 'See how much self-control I have.'" He explained that Delorme once rambled on about being like the star of *The Victim*, a current film about a priest who gave up his life to protect the secret of the confessional. On another occasion the priest had told him he would seek the arrest of a doctor, two lawyers, a notary, a merchant, and two newspaper reporters. Much to the audiences' delight, Roby began imitating the priest's gesticulations and tone: "I have made arrangements with bread and milk delivery men to act as spies for me and to record the names of their customers who spoke against me ... the truth will soon be known and I will then throw some big parties, you'll see." The audience couldn't contain its laughter and Delorme appeared extremely embarrassed.

Roby was followed by Narcisse Arcand, who testified to the excellent relationship he had with Delorme. Despite that, "he would unpredictably swing from taking me into his confidence to angrily kicking me out of the home." Delorme had once asked for his opinion on the various detectives involved, "Who do you think is the toughest?" he had asked. When the reporter replied he thought Farah-Lajoie was, Delorme replied, "Yeah, that guy is anticlerical and a womanizer. He's a great sniffer, he's got his nose stuck in everything. He carries everything off with him, even my old overshoes. He wants people to believe they were Raoul's, he even runs off with my car ... He might be smart, but he's too stupid to remove a car door he wanted to take with him. I had to do the job."

Monette then called a succession of witnesses to describe Delorme's eccentricities. One of them explained the accused's unusual method of renting out apartments, which consisted of calling all the prospective tenants together in his office and accepting the highest bid. Another, notary Jean-François Cardinal, told of having attended several parties with the priest and of being particularly intrigued with his familiarity with women, which sometimes bordered on intimacy. He described his rather odd behaviour at a party he had attended in ordering a woman he had just met to pour water into his mouth as he stood leaning on her with his hands held behind his back.

He also said that the accused had told him the pope's recent death was due to a heart attack he had suffered on hearing of the accusations against Delorme.* An officer of the Sûreté Provinciale testified that while he was accompanying Delorme to prison on the day of his arrest, the priest offered to introduce him to his sister Rosa, suggesting she would be better than the woman he had recently seen him with. Judge Monet was beginning to think that the line of evidence was getting dangerously close to providing details on Delorme's rumoured relationships with women. Interrupting the witness, he said, "I must say that if we are now going to get into evidence of the accused's immorality, I must ask all women, especially the young girls, to withdraw from the courtroom until further notice. If I had known about this, I would have given appropriate instructions earlier. I could go so far as to order a closed hearing but I won't do it because this case is of interest to the public."

The ladies left reluctantly, but they returned a short while later with reinforcements. Here is how *La Presse* described the scene:

In the afternoon they charged back in even greater numbers. The hallways were overcrowded with women of all types and all social classes – approximately thirty white-haired ladies, about a hundred mature women, as many middle-age ladies, and about forty young girls. There were women of all sizes, colour, and hairstyle. Their outfits ranged from white silk summer skirts to winter stoles of fox fur. This peculiar group besieged newspaper reporters, implored court officials, and alternatively threatened or begged entry from the policemen guarding the courtroom door. One of them told a reporter "I have come especially from New Brunswick to see him. Please arrange for me to see him if only for a second and I will leave a happy woman."

Like those everywhere else in North America, Montreal women had become much more assertive since the end of the Great War.

Despite the pressure, Judge Monet did not lift the ban and requested that the police escort the ladies out. But those who expected to hear sordid details about Delorme's alleged immorality were

---

* Pope Benedict XV died of pneumonia in January of 1922.

disappointed. Instead, they heard several of Delorme's classmates from College Ste-Thérèse tell how, despite grades lower than 40 per cent, Delorme was promoted from year to year. The reason given was that he received good marks for attendance and attention in class, which were taken into account in the overall rating. So was the frequency of taking the Sacraments of Penance and Holy Communion. On hearing this, Judge Monet asked sarcastically, "So someone who went to Holy Communion each day could do away with having to study science?" All of his former classmates were unanimous in saying that he was the college clown. During recreation periods he wouldn't mix with other students but preferred walking up and down the school balcony, dictionary in hand, making exaggerated gestures as he simulated a speech. It was acknowledged that he had a good memory and therefore did not do as badly in memory work. But he did very badly in subjects which required reasoning, such as science and philosophy. "With that record, how could he possibly have been ordained to the priesthood?" Judge Monet asked. At the convocation ceremonies Delorme created an embarrassing situation when he decided to make an impromptu speech to thank his teachers. He went on endlessly, expressing exaggerated gratitude to the point where a classmate had to stop him. The class president testified that the accused never showed the slightest emotion at his father's funeral and simply replied to his offer of condolences by saying "I will be heading up a large business." At the viewing of Raoul's remains, Delorme's main interest was to show his former classmates how he had improvised a device which kept the casket at an angle "so no one will have to rise on his toes to see Raoul's body," adding, "I intend to patent it and I'm sure the Funeral Cooperative will buy it from me."

When the first spectators arrived at the courtroom next morning, they were told there would be no hearing. Judge Monet had been confined to bed. The flu which had been bothering him for the last few days had taken a turn for the worse. Newspapers speculated that he had pneumonia and would be unable to continue on the case. His doctor ordered him to rest and the trial was adjourned until the 26 June. As the spectators milled around the courtroom door, Chief Lepage made a surprise appearance in the hallway, carrying a large package. He called over some reporters and told them it contained Delorme's racoon coat, adding, "I can prove that this coat, which Delorme accused my officers of stealing, was hidden by Delorme himself. Evidence to that effect will be provided at the proper time and place."

Despite his three-day rest, Judge Monet was still weak when the trial resumed. His illness couldn't have come at a worse time, since most of the remaining testimony concerned medical expertise and required his total concentration.

The attorney general's office had forbidden all doctors employed by the government or attached to publicly funded institutions to testify for the defence. This eliminated much of the expertise available to Delorme, but his lawyers were able to find two doctors at St-Jean-de-Dieu Hospital who were employed by the Sisters of Providence and were willing to testify. Dr De Bellefeuille, who had worked as a mental specialist at the institution for thirteen years, stressed the possible influence of heredity on Delorme's mental state. In addition to the evidence about problems on the maternal side, he pointed out that there were also probably problems on the paternal side because both of Alfred Delorme's wives had had mentally deficient children. "It is highly unlikely," said the doctor "that he would have married two women suffering from insanity." At this, the judge quipped, "Isn't marriage a matter of love more than of medicine?"

Dr De Bellefeuille said that, quite apart from the heredity factor, Delorme's behaviour showed signs of insanity. His record at Collège Ste-Thérèse was proof that there had been no "harmonious development of the different faculties which comprise one's intelligence." Although Delorme did not suffer from hallucination or illusion and could form ideas abnormally quickly, he had problems with judgment. As an example, the witness cited Delorme's comments to him: "Everything is o.k., *Bibi* will be cleared, there's nothing serious here. *Bibi* has a cassock and when you have a cassock you're protected from everything." As further evidence De Bellefeuille produced a letter that Delorme had handed him when he first visited his prison cell. After having looked it over, Judge Monet asked the clerk to read it to the jury:

My brethren: Dr Bellefeuille, Tétrault. To work for me is to work for God. To save me is to save yourselves. What an exceptional opportunity you have today! One well-placed word coming from you, a few well-placed mental restrictions which would remain your secret, coupled with your ability and your science, your reliance on God and your great love for Him. Heaven is happy with your choice, looks upon you, and depends upon you. God himself as well as his saints is joyous because the day of my delivery is near. Being in your hands facing my cause so honest, so just, and so holy. One hundred and fifteen days without saying my Mass, which was so rarely omitted for a period of twelve years. How many graces lost! How many souls in Purgatory deprived of prayers and of the sight of God? What enormous responsibility upon my false accusers. May God forgive them as I forgive them, and, notwithstanding a very great sorrow, I am completely disposed to pardon the murderer of my brother, who was so cowardly murdered.

You, my liberators, be forever blessed. You will be lucky, you will be happy. Believe me, my gratitude will be eternal as is that of all the souls that I will be able to deliver by the Masses which you will give me the joy and opportunity to say soon. Yes, all of these souls will unanimously thank God for having enlightened you to deliver me from the unjust hands of my alleged enemies. They will eternally sing of your great victory, will shower you with graces, you and yours, and will give you final perseverance. Always remember, "Help yourself and the heavens will help you." Do you forget? Never. May the Holy Spirit enlighten you and lead you!

Confidently yours.

Sincerely.

PS My greatest wish: to be at Ste-Thérèse Sunday. What a source of benediction it would be for you if you realized that great wish (of 115 days) to say the Mass. Nevertheless, may the will of God be done and not mine. Good luck.

Dr De Bellefeuille continued, "Moral sense taken by itself is insufficient to permit a diagnosis. Some of his faculties are normal, others are hypertrophied, and still others are atrophied. Some of his faculties are more atrophied than others, such as the moral sense, which in his case is extremely deficient. That reinforces my diagnosis of mental degeneracy. He cannot understand the seriousness of his trial, the evidence which might be brought against him, and the means he could use to defend himself."

He admitted that Delorme was a good speaker and had a good vocabulary, but these factors did not change his diagnosis. "Many insane people are good writers," he added. "His shrewdness and ability to deceive do not exclude insanity, as many insane people show those characteristics!"

Walsh cross-examined: "So in concluding that the accused is unfit to stand trial, you are relying exclusively on his heredity, is that right?"

"To explain the manifestations shown me, yes Sir."

"But heredity does not always mean illness, does it?"

"No sir ... what I want to say is that it is impossible to conclude the individual is insane only because of his heredity. We can't conclude he is insane only because of insanity in his family. That's impossible."

Walsh had forced the witness to contradict himself. Dr De Belle-feuille, who had earlier affirmed that the heredity factor was the most important factor in Delorme's case, had now said the exact opposite. On further questioning the witness admitted that Delorme's lack of emotion could be stoicism instead of insanity. Under the Crown's persistent questioning, Dr De Bellefeuille started to waver and his answers became less categorical. He conceded that the priest's logical behaviour regarding the will, the insurance policy, and property management showed he could understand some of what was happening around him. "Otherwise he would be an absolute idiot, which he is not."

Judge Monet joined the debate: "Do you swear under oath that in your opinion the accused does not know the meaning of murder?"

"No, your Lordship, I don't go that far."

"So then he knows its significance?"

"Perfectly."

"Do you therefore admit that he knows he is being accused of murder?"

"Yes, your Lordship."

"But you swear that the accused, although a college graduate, an ordained priest, and a professor at Collège Ste-Rose, despite all that, you swear that he is not in a state to understand the seriousness of the accusation of murder lodged against him?"

"Yes, your Lordship, as a result of my diagnosis of him I am forced to arrive at that conclusion."

"In your opinion, what did the accused want to say when he wrote the words 'with a few well-placed mental restrictions' in his letter to you?"

"Well, your Lordship, for him, proper application of justice is of relative importance in this trial and so a little mental restriction, a little lie, would be justified if it could nullify the indictment against him. In his eyes, the murder of his brother is of secondary value because he can't appreciate it in all its consequences and its seriousness. In that perspective a small mental restriction on the part of the authorities – a small trick, so to speak – could do away with that small annoyance if they cooperated. In other words, in his eyes, this whole thing is a small annoyance."

"If it is such a small annoyance for him, why did he go to the trouble of writing to Sir Lomer Gouin and Mayor Martin?"

"Well, your Lordship, two precautions are worth more than one. Better to have two barrels in your rifle than one."

"In addition to the lie?"

"Yes."

"Even the lie under oath?"

"Yes, but in his eyes that's of no importance."

"But you can't say that with certainty, can you?"

"No, I can't."

At this point, the judge reminded the witness of the Spanish theologian Sanchez who was anything but demented and who in some of his theological studies and theses had logically endorsed the proposition that mental restrictions could be justified in certain cases of murder.

The defence invited Dr Tétrault to corroborate Dr Bellefeuille's testimony. He did so unhesitatingly and was quoted by the *Toronto Globe* of 28 June as stating "I have concluded that we had to deal with a degenerate characterized by a lack of judgement and a diminution of moral sense." Visibly relieved, the defence rested its case.

The Crown's first witness was Willy Marien, the accountant retained by the Attorney General's Office to audit the Delorme estate. Delorme, who until then had appeared rather bored, started fidgeting in his seat and leaned forward several times, staring at the accountant and cupping his ear when numbers were mentioned. He often made signs of denial or smiled sarcastically at some of the amounts indicated by the witness. Marien revealed that when Alfred Delorme died in 1916 his estate was worth about $185,000, having since grown to $250,000. Raoul's income for the period from his father's death to 31 December 1921 was $41,580, against which were charged expenses of $32,000, leaving a net profit balance of $9,580. The accused's income for the same period was $43,475, against expenses of $56,387, leaving a deficit of $12,912 which, if reduced by the $3,866 he got from the exercise of his ministry, left him with a net deficit of $9,046. Marien said he could not account for what had happened to Raoul's profit of $9,580. He pointed out however that the purchase of the Franklin and trips had cost about $12,500 for the period audited. He remarked that the accused had cooperated with him during his audit but that, despite such help, he had found the bookkeeping inadequate because of the lack of vouchers, statements, and other supporting documents. Marien said that in his opinion Adélard Delorme had taken his brother's profit to cover his own deficit.

The Crown then called its expert medical witnesses, the government-appointed doctors who had been forbidden to testify for the defence. Ironically, they also concluded that Delorme was mentally deficient. Dr Carlyle Porteous, assistant medical superintendent of the Protestant hospital for the insane at Verdun, a specialist in mental diseases for close to twenty years and lecturer in mental diseases at McGill University, was firm in testifying that Delorme was of unsound mind. He was sure that Delorme's judgment was insufficient for him to stand trial. He said the accused couldn't advise his lawyers any more than could a child of twelve. His testimony undoubtedly carried added weight with the totally French Canadian Catholic jury because he was an English Canadian Protestant testifying for the Crown but nevertheless helping the defence of a French Canadian Catholic priest.

Dr Omer Noël, assistant medical supervisor at l'Hôpital Saint-Jean-de-Dieu, gave much the same information. He had been part of a group of five doctors who had jointly examined Delorme. By this time the similarity of the doctors' testimony had aroused Judge Monet's suspicions. When he learned that Noël had not personally studied Delorme's file and was relying on hearsay to lecture the court on the accused's childish state of mind, the judge admonished him. A few minutes later, when it became clear that Noël had not even read the accused's deposition on which he was basing his expertise, the judge got furious. He told the witness he was incompetent, better qualified to be a street cleaner than a doctor, and dishonourably discharged him from the stand.

Dr Camille Laviolette didn't improve matters when he told the court that Delorme showed a lack of will-power and moral sense in disregarding the Archdiocese's directions to exercise his ministry. Judge Monet impatiently interrupted: "How can you consider that a proof of insanity?"

"Given that he is a priest, your Lordship, given his training, his vocation, a profession which should have trained him for a lifetime of work, of self-sacrifice, exemplary conduct, modesty, etc., he nevertheless appears to have ignored all that and to be too weak willed to carry out his duty. He prefers to follow his inclinations."

"But, doesn't that simply mean that he wasn't a good priest? Does it necessarily mean he was insane?"

"It means, your Lordship, that he lacked a moral sense."

"But aren't there many people without a moral sense who are not insane?"

"Yes, your Lordship."

When the witness brought up the heredity factor to explain Delorme's insanity, the judge reminded him of Rosa's case: "Since the accused's natural sister Rosa Delorme showed no sign of insanity, could you not conclude, as other doctors have, that the heredity factor could have jumped a generation in this case?"

"It's possible, your Lordship, it's possible."

"Is it just as possible for the accused as it has been for Rosa?"

"Certainly."

By now, convinced that the doctors had closed ranks in their diagnosis, Judge Monet was determined to show the other side of the equation. This meant he would have to in effect cross-examine them. He braced himself for a contest when Dr Donald MacTaggart, professor of medical jurisprudence at McGill (and one of the doctors who had performed the autopsy on Raoul), was called to the stand. It was with a great sense of relief that he listened as the doctor said, "It appears to me that a man who has completed a classical course, followed by a theological course, although it may have taken him a greater number of years to follow that course, cannot be entirely lacking in intelligence."

Following Laviolette's testimony the Crown requested that Delorme's testimony at the coroner's inquest be read into the record. The defence objected, claiming such evidence was inadmissible because it was given by the accused without his having been cautioned that it might be used against him. It also insisted that to allow the testimony would violate the rule that the accused could not be compelled to testify. The objection was overruled. Judge Monet held that if the trial were on the merits of the accusation, the point might be open to discussion. However, such was not the case, he said. "The purpose of the deposition is to determine whether or not it might reveal signs of insanity in the accused," he insisted, "not to determine his guilt or innocence." Turning to the jury, he explained that his decision should in no way be considered as incriminating Delorme on the charge of murder. "He's as white as snow and must remain so until such time as he's found guilty." For two hours the court listened attentively as the clerk read the deposition. Its lucidity certainly suggested that it had been given by a sane person. The accused also hung on every word and by the time the reading was over, he looked utterly exhausted. Walsh didn't say anything. He thought the quality of the deposition spoke for itself. But the judge wasn't through. To hammer his point home he recalled Dr De Bellefeuille to the stand.

"Now, doctor, can you say, backed by the theory you explained in your earlier testimony, that the man giving such an absolutely irreproachable testimony from every point of view can be considered as an imbecile, insane, and unfit to stand trial – can you tell me in what circumstances a man accused of murder could stand trial?"

"Evidently, when there isn't a serious gap in his intelligence. An individual can be more or less intelligent but the compass in matters of intellect is judgment and moral sense."

"What lack of compass is there in what you just heard?"

"None."

The Crown's evidence was complete. Judge Monet adjourned until the following morning, but first lifted his ban on women. "I was considered to be something of a barbarian for excluding women from the court. I did it because, after consulting the accused's lawyers, I thought there would be evidence of immorality. Since I thought it would be improper to allow women to attend, I asked them to leave. Some obeyed, but we had to ask the police to escort others out. Since the evidence is now terminated I lift the ban. Ladies will be allowed in court tomorrow."

As the lawyers chatted and shuffled their papers back into their briefcases, Chief Lepage approached Walsh and handed him an affidavit signed by Reverend Sister Marie-Madeleine of the Little Daughters of St Joseph. Walsh smiled as he read the document. It stated that Delorme himself had brought his racoon coat to their convent for repair on 13 February. The affidavit continued: "Having read in the newspapers that the coat had been stolen and that certain detectives were suspected of having done so, we decided to notify the authorities that we have the coat. It and a cassock which was also brought in for repair were handed over to detectives Pigeon and Gauthier of the Montreal Police Force on 22 June 1922." This certainly made a liar of Delorme. Why did the coat need repairs? And wasn't it a strange coincidence that he brought it to the convent on the day he learned he would be arrested? And why did the Little Daughters of St Joseph wait so long before turning it over to the authorities?

The atmosphere in the courtroom next morning, 30 June, can best be described by quoting the *Montreal Daily Star*:

It was a gala day in the court room. Information had mysteriously spread throughout the city that the ban on women would be lifted. They took full advantage of it. By 9:30 the Delorme sisters and their aunt were in their places; by 9:45 the entire section of seats reserved for women was filled and overflowing, one section, however, being kept for a party of Mr Justice Monet's relatives. A conspicuous spectator was a boy of about eight years who accompanied his mother. He was the first "man" to arrive, but he was not far ahead of others who swarmed into court, filled seats and aisles, stood on window ledges, and overflowed into the lawyer's enclave. There was an unusual number of lawyers, many of whom, with more free time now that the civil court term had ended, had gathered to hear the argument, especially the judge's charge.

What Mr Justice Monet would say excited the keenest interest. It was reported that he would speak for one and a half to two hours.

When Delorme reached the corridor leading to the dock he stopped for a moment to smile and gaily salute his family. He appeared in a court bright with the varied colours of women's hats and gowns and filled to suffocation.

As he took the bench, Judge Monet referred to a report in *Le Canada* that some doctors had met the previous evening to protest his treatment of Dr Noël. "Speaking for the dignity of the bench, I must say that a judge does not have to justify the relevancy of his questions. Certain doctors criticized some of the questions I asked Dr Noël. I would beg the doctors, at least those who are respectable and to whom respect is due, to consider that as far as I am concerned one sparrow does not a summer make, nor does one doctor, who I think is a fool, incriminate his fellow doctors who are intelligent. The doctors who are here surely have a good knowledge of literature and must be familiar with these words of Boileau, known as the poet of reason: 'And so, to end with a small touch of satire, A fool always finds a bigger fool as admirer.'"*

He then invited the lawyers to make their closing arguments. Everyone looked forward to brilliant oratory from two of the city's most prominent lawyers. Among other things, the Delorme trial had become a popular learning tool for Montreal law students, many of whom would rush down to the court house after their afternoon classes. Most of them were there, virtually sitting on each other's laps in a small area which the judge had set aside for the classmates of his son, Fabio. There was a general feeling that those who had been lucky enough to be admitted to the courtroom would be among the privileged few to witness the conclusion of the most controversial case in Canadian judicial history.

Expectation changed to astonishment when both lawyers declined to make any closing argument and, breaking with tradition, said they

* "Eh, bien, pour finir, par un trait de satire,
  Un fou trouve toujours un plus fou qui l'admire."

preferred to rely entirely on the judge's address. Startled, Judge
Monet replied, "Gentlemen of the jury, I am perhaps the most
surprised person in this courtroom. I am as anxious to finish as you
are, but we must end this trial intelligently. Since it is only 11:20, I
will adjourn until 2:00 this afternoon to reflect on all this and prepare
as clear and as accurate an address as I can."

Judge Monet's address lasted forty-five minutes and was described
by the press as "perhaps one of the most sensational ever delivered in
a Canadian Criminal Court." With tears in his eyes, he first addressed
the lawyers: "I will remember for a long time, perhaps forever, the
mark of confidence you have just given me. While I appreciate your
confidence in me, I recognize the responsibility it entails." Turning
towards the jury, he continued, "the case before you, gentlemen of
the jury, is not only extraordinary, but one of the two or three most
important cases ever to unfold before a Court of Criminal Assizes."

Observing that only two priests had ever been accused of murder,
a German-American and a priest who had been guillotined in France,
he continued: "You heard the evidence. Unless I am gravely mistaken,
you have already formed an opinion. I would venture to guess that it
is different from mine. You have your duty, I have mine. You have
taken an oath to render a verdict according to the evidence you have
heard. The accused is a priest, but whatever an accused may be, a
lawyer, doctor, notary, a member of any other profession, even a
judge, he must be considered simply as an accused."

He recalled that certain people had been offended by similar
remarks he had made to the jury panel at the start of the trial and
singled out the two priests who had felt it necessary to write him.
"One, a person whose name I will reveal because he was a witness
here, was Father Lachapelle, chaplain of Bordeaux Prison. I won't
mention the name of the other. The only reason I refer to these letters
is that I believe they represent the mentality of a certain part of our
population and maybe, just maybe, some of you feel the same way.
Please note that among the two to three thousand priests in the
Province of Quebec, only two felt they should dictate my judgment.
I thank all the other members of the clergy who, in a case as important
as this one, refrained from giving me advice. One of the priests wrote
this sublime passage: "Poor judge, you're pitiful. You should learn
your catechism." Now listen to his conclusion: "You are unworthy to
sit on the Bench and should come down from it as soon as possible."
Judge Monet looked coldly at the jury and in a slow deliberate voice
said: "Gentlemen, I have too much respect for myself to answer those

types of letters and insults and I will tell you frankly that I simply threw that piece of literary spittle into my spittoon."

The judge then read an extract from Father Lachapelle's letter: "The newspapers quote you as making an error in religious doctrine which I believe you should correct because our people can't believe that a judge is ignorant of his catechism to that extent." He said, "I do not ignore my catechism to that extent. I am a Roman Catholic, as you are, gentlemen, and I pride myself not only on believing in my religion but on openly practising it. I had the privilege of attending a priest's ordination on at least ten different occasions. During that ceremony the postulant is told '*tu es sacerdos in aeternum*, – you are a priest for eternity.' And at the end of the ceremony 'you are another Christ, another Christ, *tu es alter Christus.*' But I could not allow myself, either in my remarks before the grand jury or before you, to associate the name of Jesus Christ with someone presently accused of one of the most monstrous crimes committed in a civilized country since Cain." On hearing this, Delorme who had been casually leaning on the prisoner's rail, turned bright red, gave the judge a menacing look, and abruptly dropped to his seat.

The judge read on: "Our Lord and his mother respected Judas despite his betrayal. I know that," Judge Monet added, "but Judas hanged himself after betraying his Master and despite this horrible self-inflicted punishment, despite a generous pardon by Christ and his Mother, never before Father Lachapelle has a man dared suggest that Iscariot was entitled to be called Reverend."

Judge Monet then returned to the main issue. "The only question before us today is, is the accused mentally capable of being tried? There are only three points to consider. Is he aware of what is happening around him? Can he understand what is happening around him? Do his mental faculties permit him to tell his lawyers whether or not he has committed the crime and what means of defence are available to him?"

Reviewing the evidence, he began with the accused's behaviour at school. "Do you think it is sign of insanity for a weaker student to study while his classmates are playing? I leave that to your appreciation. What did the authorities of Collège Ste-Thérèse say? They declared that he was sufficiently intelligent to be ordained a priest and furthermore to be a professor at their institution. Imagine the archbishop of Montreal, whose opinion, I would think, is worth that of three classmates, saying to this man: 'You are qualified for the priesthood. You will have the right to consecrate. You will have the right to ask Christ to come into the Host.' Would the Church have conferred that right on a buffoon?"

Next, the judge reviewed Handfield's "farfetched" testimony. "How could this man associate with the accused for more than four years if he knew from the start that he was an idiot? According to Handfield, everyone considered him demented. Despite that, he would chat with him, not just for a casual minute or so but sometimes for as long as an hour and a half. It was obvious that he didn't consider Delorme insane when he offered to be his travelling companion. I leave it to you, gentlemen of the jury, to decide who in those circumstances was the bigger fool."

Commenting on the medical expertise, he said that in the final analysis all of the qualified doctors had found Delorme to have a normal degree of awareness, memory, and will. "Awareness," he said, "allowed Delorme to understand what is happening at his trial, memory allowed him to remember what happened in the past, and will allowed him to choose right from wrong. So, gentlemen, here's an accused who possesses the three faculties required to be human. And if the accused has those three faculties to such a high degree, how can you conclude that he can't understand what constitutes murder, especially that of his brother? How can he not understand the meaning of the testimony he heard? If he is aware of things, can want them and remember them, how can you possibly conclude that he doesn't have enough sense to help his lawyers prepare his defence?"

Judge Monet's final remarks concerned his unusually active participation in the trial. "My actions were justified because of newspaper reports that the trial was a put-up job and that the verdict was already decided. Gentlemen, I accepted this case reluctantly. I even asked my chief justice to replace me as presiding judge. I am a Roman Catholic like the accused and I hoped to be relieved of a burden I didn't want to bear. But I was told to be at my post, so I am, and I carried out my duty to the best of my knowledge. I acted as I did because this case is of interest not only on this continent but has crossed the oceans and will have worldwide repercussions. For generations to come, people will ask, everywhere, 'what happened in the Delorme case?' I want to be sure the world knows that here in the province of Quebec, here in Canada as elsewhere, a judge is aware that, like Caesar's wife, he must be above all suspicion."

Before sending the jury out to deliberate, Judge Monet once again explained the nature of the defence's preliminary plea of insanity. Since Delorme was not being tried on the murder charge, the usual rule of giving the accused the benefit of the doubt didn't apply, but nevertheless the jury had to be unanimous in its verdict. "I ask you to reach a conclusion which is reasonable, logical, and honest."

The crowded and tense courtroom quietly awaited the jury's return. After twenty minutes, they shuffled back to their seats. The court usher announced the judge's entrance. Delorme was led to his seat. He leaned forward in his chair. Each juror responded to the call of his name. The judge ordered the prisoner to stand. The audience held its breath.

The clerk called out: "Do you believe that the prisoner is mentally incapable of being tried for murder, yes or no?" Without a moment's hesitation, the jurors simultaneously and loudly answered: "Yes."

Judge Monet smiled. He had expected that verdict. "Gentlemen of the jury, I'm sure I don't have to tell you that the court always respects a jury's verdict, regardless of whether or not it agrees with it. I sincerely believe that you rendered yours in accordance with your conviction as twelve honest men. I must now tell you that a different verdict might have been less severe for the accused. The law requires that I ask the authorities to keep him in custody and that I make a report to the lieutenant governor, who will then tell me in which mental institution the accused must spend the rest of his days. Frankly, I believe you did your duty and will be happy to leave the courtroom. You are released and so am I. I think we will all have a good night's sleep – we deserve it." Escorted by two policemen, Delorme was led away. Judge Monet bowed to the audience, praised the lawyers and retired to his chambers, completely exhausted. Throughout most of the trial he had exerted himself beyond human limit, totally disregarding his doctor's orders to suspend proceedings and recover from the flu which had been plaguing him.*

The verdict made front page headlines across the nation. Delorme's flock of supporters was delighted. Many others rejected the insanity verdict and demanded a trial for murder. It was unbelievable to them that the jury had taken only nineteen minutes to resolve such a complex issue. Under the headline "*Is Delorme Really Insane?*" *Le Bulletin* editorialized:

Will the verdict in the Delorme case satisfy public opinion? The answer is a categorical "no." All we can say is that perhaps 10% of the population is satisfied. We need only listen to conversations in the street, in the taverns,

---

* A few months later, Judge Monet took a Caribbean cruise on his doctor's orders. He died of a heart attack on board the *ss Megantic*.

in public buildings and work centers. Since the beginning of the trial, public opinion has been definite that Delorme was not insane. That same public, with its good common sense will not accept a verdict so opposed to reality. Delorme is not insane and has never been. Here is a man who completes his "cours classique," his theology course, is ordained a priest, is named professor in a classical college, practises his ministry for ten years, has the confidence of the Church, and is then considered insane? Really! Let's put things in perspective and ask ourselves if the people who accepted him as intelligent and gave him responsible functions are also crazy. His father, who followed his progress very closely, would also have had to have been an imbecile to have appointed him the executor of a fortune valued at a quarter of a million dollars. A man like the accused's father, successful in amassing such a colossal fortune, must certainly be something other than an imbecile. We must assume that his intelligence was sufficient to distinguish a fool from an intelligent person. It would have been easy for him to find others who could serve as executors rather than entrust the management of his fortune to someone he considered to be an idiot. He was insane at birth, declared the experts. Delorme is not insane, answered the public, and it says it again today. He's a degenerate, he's amoral, he's boastful, he's vain, he's conceited, he's avaricious, but he is not a fool.

The jury came under heavy fire when another publication asked:

What is the significance of an insanity trial which is decided by a jury made up of unsophisticated and ignorant men, unqualified to judge psychological matters? While it might be acceptable to make them the ultimate judges of facts when the issues are straightforward, it is unacceptable that such men, wearing the heavy boots of a garbage collector or stevedore, should enter the delicate realm of abstractions. During the Middle Ages an accused was judged by his peers, a baron by barons, an apothecary by those adept with pestle and mortar, etc. We have now fallen behind the Middle Ages. We have not recognized that we cannot involve ourselves in things which are absurd and unrealistic without repercussion. When one finger is caught in the net, the whole body follows."

Suggestions of outside influence were made and there was growing concern over how English and Protestant Canada would judge the administration of justice in Quebec.

Trying to interfere with justice will be costly for Quebec. Our adversaries will throw this odious stone at our heads far more often than we would wish.

However much we affirm our loyalty and show our tolerance, we will forever be reproached for this shameful favouritism. Even if we were all to become fountains of knowledge, our values would still be called into question. The legend will spread that in our *collèges classiques*, good grades are obtained because of good conduct alone and that the teachers of our young are insane. And as naive as these superficial appearances may be, they will still cause us humiliation. What will be thought of our moral sense – which deserves more respect than Delorme's non-existent one – if we so publicly advertise our contempt for the common rule of justice? Will we be taken seriously in the Dominion, if we act with such levity?

Delorme's insanity has been established on the basis of inaccurate explorations of the Delorme family's past, with reports of senile madness, maternity fevers, and alcoholic degeneracy all exploited to the accused's benefit. The father of all these alleged idiots, Adélard, Florence, and Lilly, was nevertheless intelligent enough, despite a limited education, to build up a fortune of a quarter of a million dollars.

We can only deplore the clumsy zeal of those fanatics who, to save a gangrened limb, have sacrificed the whole body. We find it incompetent to have accused Delorme of a crime and to then attempt to prove his innocence by means of an insanity plea available because of legal technicalities. We have achieved a result which was unforseen by all the pseudo-psychologists – many who originally doubted the priest's guilt now firmly believe in it and many others who considered the accused to be a degenerate and an imbecile now consider him to be *compos mentis*. The moral of all this was best said by Lafontaine: "better a wise enemy than a fool for a friend."*

The medical journal *L'Indépendance médicale* took issue with some of the medical expertise, but not without directing some criticism at the legal profession and judicial system.

Before his arrest, Delorme reasoned and discussed things in a logical manner. At the coroner's inquest he testified with remarkable clarity and precision. But suddenly, since his incarceration, especially since he had been in contact with his lawyers, he became a cautious mute!

A degenerate, he was. There is no doubt of that. But a degenerate is not inevitably an irresponsible person. If society were to lock up all the degenerates, it would have to create huge asylums. We rub shoulders with many of them every day in the street, in the streetcars, and in the suburbs. There

* "Mieux vaut un sage ennemi qu'un sot ami."

are even some who are mentally deficient throughout their lives, yet occupy functions and jobs at the top of the social ladder!

The verdict of those twelve citizens is as illogical as the criminal law that permits a medical question in a legal case such as that of the Reverend Delorme to be decided by persons of limited knowledge whose intelligence is a wasteland and whose judgment is deficient. Their verdict has not satisfied public opinion, to say nothing of medical opinion.

Despite its quasi-unanimous censure of the jury system, the media had nothing but praise for Judge Monet. At various times throughout the trial his conduct had been attacked by members of the clergy, the medical profession and the media. But by the time the verdict came down, public opinion was on his side. *The Montreal Herald* editorialized:

Mr. Justice Monet
As was anticipated by the large majority of people, the jury yesterday declared that the Rev. J. Adélard Delorme was mentally unfit to stand trial on the charge of murder.

So, for the time being at any rate, the case sinks into oblivion, although there is, of course, the possibility that it will be re-opened, as it must be according to the law of the land, should the accused man be declared mentally fit to face the charge.

The case is, therefore, still *sub judice*,* and comment is not permissible. The *Herald*, however, wishes to record its opinion on one feature of the recent inquiry, and that is the conduct of the proceedings by Mr Justice Monet. Our readers will be well advised to study his charge to the jury. It is one of the most remarkable ever made in this or any other country. It discloses the terrible difficulties that have surrounded the case from the outset, and the almost super-human task that the Judge was called upon to face.

His charge was eloquent in the extreme, full of pathos, and delivered with a heartfelt sense of his responsibility.

Mr Justice Monet's conduct of the case throughout left nothing to be desired. Never did he lose sight of the responsibility of his office, and whatever may be the general opinion as to the correctness of the verdict, the public recognizes that the case was conducted without fear or favour with but one object in view – to render justice.

* Before the court.

Mr Justice Monet has, by his handling of the case, added to the high reputation of the Canadian Bench, and he is deserving of the highest praise. Of him well may it be said that he has fulfilled Wolsey's advice to Cromwell:
Be just and fear not:
Let all the ends thou aim'st at be thy country's,
Thy God's, and truth's.

In a 4 July 1922 editorial, the *Toronto Evening Telegram* stated:

The Courage of Judge Monet.
No feature of the Delorme case has been more amazing than the stress which the presiding Judge saw fit to lay upon his duty to subject a priest to the same legal procedure as if he had been a layman. It did not require Judge Monet's announcement that he had sought to be excused from the Delorme case for one to realize how acutely he must have felt the embarrassment of hearing a murder charge against a cleric of his own religion. Judge Monet did a brave thing; his bravery consisted in boldly affirming the law of this land that the State may not bow to the temporal power of any church.

That authority was challenged. From an abbé of Judge Monet's faith came an admonition to consult his catechism – not his law books – to see whether he was not guilty of impiety in considering an accused priest as a private citizen. "You are unworthy of the Bench," concluded his reverend critic, "and should descend as soon as possible."

Judge Monet, himself a French-Canadian and a Roman Catholic, threw the Abbé's letter into the cuspidor, but the spirit which breathes in every syllable of that epistle cannot be so easily exorcized. It is a letter which epitomizes in few and simple words the age-long story of the struggle between the Church and the State. One or the other must be supreme; there can be neither compromise nor co-equality. The revelations of the Delorme case have shown up in bold relief the conflicts in which Canada is involved, and thereby is supplied the evidence upon which Quebec, as well as the other provinces, can reach a deliberate and intelligent decision.

In the days that followed, Delorme was moved from Montreal to the St Michel Archange hospital near Quebec city. He was allowed no visitors without the attorney general's written authorization. Surprisingly, after the initial outcry against the verdict, the case quickly drifted out of public attention. Could it be that with Delorme out of sight the Church and state could quietly work behind the scenes to have him stand trial? There were even rumours that the Vatican was getting involved. L'affaire Delorme had become an embarrassment. The general view was that justice was not being served because Delorme was a priest. Both Church and state authorities wanted to dispel that view by having him stand trial for murder like any other citizen.

Farah-Lajoie decided that the case had to be resolved. He wrote a booklet entitled *Ma version de l'Affaire Delorme* and approached Montreal publishing companies with his manuscript. None of them was interested. It was finally published in Toronto by the Central News and Publishing Company. The book reviewed his investigation, summarized the trial, and clearly condemned the priest. In his preface, he explained:

One might ask: why publish facts that many people would like to forget. Why make myself the judge of this case and give a somewhat official tone to what might simply be a personal whim? My answer is that this modest booklet has two objectives. The first, and most important, is to reestablish certain facts which have been distorted by rumours and to tell the truth, once and for all. The second is personal. Time and again I have been accused either of negligence or zealousness. My name has been associated with offensive and unmerited epithets. I have been accused of odd and unlikely crimes, such as the theft of a coat, and also with more serious and unjust things, such as having been bribed. Because the verdict of insanity handed down against Delorme has protected an individual who should be under arrest, I believe that having accomplished my duty this far it is only fitting that I accomplish it to the very end. This little booklet will at least show the public that the Montreal Police understands its duty and scrupulously carries it out, sometimes despite extraordinary obstacles.

The booklet sold like hot cakes to everyone but the clergy. The Roman Catholic Church banned it. The order form received by the Archdiocese of Montreal contains this handwritten note scrawled across the front, "We want nothing to do with this book, written by such a man."

During this period Delorme's legal status was somewhat ambiguous, to say the least. Although he had been found criminally insane, under civil law he could still act as administrator of his father's and Raoul's estates. But who would take the risk of dealing with him? The only way for this to be corrected was for him to be interdicted for insanity and a curator appointed to manage the estates. The curator chosen was his brother-in-law, Adélard Tétrault. A petition was presented to the Superior Court by Delorme's lawyer Gustave Monette. Delorme wouldn't have it. He would not be denied his cherished authority over the family assets. He revoked Monette's mandate and appointed Léopold Houle as his lawyer with instructions "to protest with all your strength any attempt at interdiction which would prohibit me from managing my affairs, my assets." Despite this, Monette persisted with his petition. What was expected to be a mere formality turned into a quagmire when Delorme's lawyer asked Dr Brochu, superintendent of St Michel Archange hospital, to certify his client's insanity. Not only did Brochu refuse to do so, but a few weeks later, on 7 September, he issued the following certificate:

I, the undersigned, medical superintendent of Hôpital St Michel Archange, certify that Father Adélard Delorme of Montreal, presently interned in this hospital for reasons of insanity and on order of the Lieutenant Governor in Council, has not shown any evident signs of imbecility, insanity, or madness since the first day of his internment and I am of the opinion that his state of mental lucidity is sufficient to allow him to manage his business affairs, care for his person, and choose a lawyer.

Dr D. Brochu

How could one reconcile this with the earlier verdict? By stating that Delorme had not shown any signs of insanity since the day of his internment, which followed the jury's verdict by a matter of days, Brochu was saying the jury was wrong. This infuriated a large part of the population, which felt Quebec was being made a laughing stock. In its 12 October 1922 lead editorial entitled "Le Scandale Delorme," *Le Canada* stated:

One should not be surprised that these successive happenings have led the public to believe that someone wanted to protect the accused and impede legal process. At the present time, the Delorme case is considered to be one of the most scandalous in the annals of justice. If we want justice to be respected, we must believe that it treats us all equally and that neither the cassock nor the use of influence can be anyone's protector.

Delorme used Brochu's certificate in his attempt to be released on a writ of habeas corpus. Despite Brochu's opinion, on 16 November 1922 Delorme was civilly interdicted and his brother-in-law Tétrault appointed as his curator. The court ruled that the administration of the Delorme estate could not be left in such a confused state and, considering Tétrault's experience as a bank manager, appointed him as the person of authority.

Furious, Delorme changed attorneys once again. A few months later, his new lawyer, Alleyn Taschereau, KC, a prominent criminal

lawyer from Quebec City, submitted Brochu's certificate to Lieutenant Governor Charles Fitzpatrick.* To everyone's surprise, on 23 May
1923 the lieutenant governor declared Delorme fit for trial and
returned him to Bordeaux Prison. One problem had been exchanged
for another: he was now criminally sane but civilly insane, a situation
which would cause more problems as time went on.†

---

* Alleyn Taschereau was not related to the prime minister and attorney general of the
  same name.
† Somewhere along the way, Dr Brochu was retired from his job, apparently because
  of his controversial certificate. In its 17 April 1923 edition, the *Toronto Sentinel*
  published the following report:
  "Another phase in the Delorme case is developing," says the *Toronto Telegram* in
  discussing the matter. Dr Brochu, superintendent of the Beauport Asylum where
  Delorme has been interned since having been declared insane, is to be retired
  from his position shortly. Should his successor be named before Delorme's release,
  a change of diagnosis is possible. Brochu has insisted from the outset that Delorme
  is quite sane and competent to stand trial and has aroused hostility from certain
  officials and ecclesiastical sources for his statements on the subject. It is well known
  that the Roman Catholic Church authorities are vigorously opposed to Delorme's
  liberation as it will precipitate an avalanche of fresh gossip after the case had more
  or less faded from public memory. The Church would then be faced with the
  problem of permitting Delorme to roam the city in his religious garb or he would
  have to be unfrocked, an act that might appear prejudicial to Delorme in the
  public view.

The Evidence

On 11 June 1923 Delorme appeared before the associate chief justice of the King's Bench, G.E. Martin, to have his trial fixed. The defence had been joined by a new counsel. Next to Alleyn Taschereau sat the distinguished Charles Hazlett Cahan, KC.* Such a distinguished Anglo-Saxon Protestant coming to the defence of Delorme would certainly impress the jury which, it was anticipated, would include members of Montreal's English Protestant community.† Widespread media criticism of the Catholic jury's "shameful favouritism" and "illogical" verdict at the insanity trial made this almost a foregone conclusion.

---

* Born in Nova Scotia, the sixty-two-year-old Cahan had practised in Halifax for fourteen years before moving to Montreal and becoming a member of the Quebec Bar in 1907. By the time of his sudden death in 1944 at the age of eighty-two, Cahan had attained the summit in law, business, politics, and diplomacy. He was a prodigious worker. His achievements included several doctorates in law; secretary of state for Canada during the Bennett administration; the organisation of hydroelectric plants and urban transportation systems in Central America during the course of which he became the confident of Porfirio Diaz, president of Mexico; Canadian negotiator for the settlement of the Canada-German war debt in 1918; Canada's principal delegate at the 1932 meeting of the League of Nations in Geneva; and diplomatic missions to Japan and China. He was a member of the Bar Association of New York City, the Royal Empire Society of London, the Canadian Club, the University and Bankers Club of New York, the Ottawa Rideau Club, and the Mount Royal Club, to name a few.

† The 1921 official Census reveals the following racial and religious classification of Montreal's population.

Racial		Religious	
French	63%	Roman Catholic	75%
British	31%	Protestant	17%
Other	6%	Jewish	7%
		Other	1%

A battle erupted when Delorme was asked how he pled to the charge of murder. Neither Cahan nor Taschereau replied. Instead Gustave Monette rose and told the court that the accused "was not fit to be tried." Cahan jumped up, saying that he represented Delorme and would not allow anyone else to speak for him. The lawyers exchanged angry words. When order was restored, Robert Louis Calder,* the crown prosecutor, said he didn't care who represented Delorme as long as someone did. The clerk repeated the charge. Once again, Monette shot up and pleaded not guilty. Furious, Delorme shouted, "I will do the answering here and I am, Sir, not guilty." Monette insisted that his plea of insanity be entered in the record. "I represent the accused at the request of his curator and I have the right to have a plea recorded." On hearing this, Delorme was beside himself with rage. "I have no curator," he shrieked, "and I don't want his lawyers." Another heated exchange followed between the lawyers and the judge, throughout which Delorme grunted, groaned, and smiled incredulously. Finally Judge Martin rejected Monette's plea and fixed the trial date for Wednesday, 20 June.

There was more order once the trial began. Officials had devised controls to exclude everyone from the Assizes until all of the lawyers, witnesses, jurymen, reporters, and other interested parties had been seated and special entrance permits had been issued. Policemen lined the hallways and a chain, strung across the courtroom door, was guarded by four policemen who checked all permits before allowing anyone in. As reported on page 1 of the 23 June edition of the *Toronto Globe*, "An unusual feature of the trial is the entanglement of newspaper cameras which has completely blocked the passageway in the fight to secure exclusive court scenes. The granting of permission to photographers to interrupt or distract proceedings is said to be without precedent."

The courtroom was squeaky clean. The occasion had justified a thorough facelift, including a fresh coat of paint and a thorough washing of the windows. The curtains had been washed and the copper accessories, from the railings to the ink wells and spittoons, glistened. The large crucifix hanging on the courtroom wall had also

---

* Robert Louis Calder, KC had been impressive in many important criminal trials. Forty-five years of age and a Roman Catholic, he carried himself with the self-assurance of a military commander. Indeed he had been decorated with the Military Cross in 1918 for conspicuous service at the battle of Amiens. Active in the young socialist CCF party, he participated in many public debates, one of which was a famous contest held at Montreal's His Majesty's Theatre against the renowned American lawyer Clarence Darrow on the question of capital punishment.

been spotlessly polished. All of the courtroom officials and policemen were in their full-dress uniforms. Here is how the *Montreal Gazette* of Wednesday morning, 20 June, described the scene under the heading "Pomp of Law Will Mark Great Trial":

Pomp and ceremony, such as never have been witnessed before here in a court of justice, will mark the opening of the trial for murder of Rev. Father Adélard Delorme this morning in the Court of King's Bench. The large stairway of the court house will be lined with provincial constables in uniforms, and all traffic will be stopped until the court opens.

A few minutes before 10 o'clock (standard time) a procession will be formed, consisting of the Sheriff of Montreal, Dr F.Y. Lemieux, the lawyers in the case, a number of court officials and criers and a squad of policemen. They will call for Chief Justice Sir François Lemieux who will come out from the room of Mr Justice Archer on the third floor of the building.

The Chief Justice who will wear the robes and three cornered hat of his office, will be escorted in solemn procession down the broad stairway, the sheriff following, wearing his uniform and sword. Behind will follow the Crown prosecutor, R.L. Calder, KC, the lawyers for the defence, in all probability, the clerk of the Crown, Mr E.A.B. Ladouceur, and a host of minor officials.

The ceremony has been especially ordered by the sheriff, and strict instructions have been given to keep all outsiders away. Placards were prepared yesterday afternoon, bearing the "No Admission" legend in French and English. They will be posted on the doors of the courtroom. Tickets have been issued to the few who are to be admitted.

The fact that 180 jurymen will be present excludes the onlookers who haunted the court during the last trial of the priest. Only lawyers who have some connection with the case, the court officials assigned and one representative from each local newspaper will be admitted.

When the court opens there will be two judges on the bench. Chief Justices Sir François Lemieux and Martin. The latter will formally greet his colleague from Quebec, then retire, and Delorme will hear the indictment read."

At seventy-two, Lemieux's vast experience – which included acting as defence counsel for Louis Riel* – made him one of the best criminal jurists in the country. When he was in private practice one could often hear: "If anyone can cheat the gallows, it is François Xavier Lemieux." Now getting on in years, he would have preferred not to have to preside over the controversial Delorme trial.

---

* Louis Riel was hanged for treason in 1885.

Judge Lemieux addressed the audience: "At the request of my friend the Honourable Associate Chief Justice Martin I accepted the formidable task of presiding at the Delorme trial. I come here with confidence, convinced that I will discharge my duty impartially and render justice to all concerned. I ask the press to be discreet in its reporting of these proceedings. I count on the courage and intelligence of the jury, the enlightenment of the lawyers, and Providence."

Calder ordered the sheriff to bring in the accused. Well-groomed, and proudly wearing his usual black suit, Delorme looked confidently around the court room as he was led in to the prisoner's dock. No sooner had the clerk read the charge than the ever present Monette interjected, "I appear before this court on behalf of a third party who has an important duty to discharge. By law, the curator is responsible for the person of the accused. He has asked me to point out to the court, for the record, that six specialists in mental disease have declared him to be completely insane. Although the lieutenant governor ordered a new trial, the court must hold a preliminary hearing on the accused's mental state." Delorme's counsel replied that Delorme was fit to defend himself. "The prisoner at the bar is entitled to a trial," said Cahan "Our laws give him that right. It is in the interest of justice that he be tried in order to put an end to this scandal." After a short deliberation the judge ruled that "the lieutenant governor declared the accused mentally fit. Our duty is to try him. To do otherwise would constitute a refusal to give him justice, a task we are here to facilitate, not hinder." The *Toronto Globe* later quoted the judge as having said that the insanity plea was "plausible to anyone not knowing the law."

The jury had yet to be chosen and be sworn. Close to 200 candidates had been called and two arbitrators would decide on the competence of each. The defence was particularly cautious in its choice of English-speaking Protestants. It certainly didn't want any anti-Catholics. If there was to be a bias, it preferred to select someone who would be reluctant to condemn a Roman Catholic priest for fear of being labelled a bigot. The whole affair was very delicate. Finally, by seven o'clock that evening, a jury of eight French Canadians and four English Canadians had been chosen.* After appropriate arrange-

---

* The jury consisted of William Hughes, Emeril Duranceau, Georges Corriveau, H.F.B. Powell, G.S. Tiffany, Alfred Plourde, Alexis Provost, William Niddle, Jules Goyer, Wilfrid David, Daniel Guimond, and P. Décarie.

ments were made for translation, the judge adjourned until next morning.*

When the trial resumed on Thursday, Sir François Lemieux remarked to the jury that "the accused, Adélard Delorme, is before you accused of the murder of Raoul Delorme in Montreal on or about 6 or 7 January 1922. The accused has pleaded not guilty to that charge and so has placed the matter in the hands of his country, which you represent. It is therefore your duty to faithfully enquire if the accused is guilty or not. You must remain together to hear the evidence."

At the request of the lawyers, he asked all witnesses to leave the room and invited the attorneys to make their opening statements. Calder explained his approach. He would first establish the motive for the crime, then prove that Adélard had shot Raoul at home and raced out to Snowdon to dispose of the body.

The Crown's first witness was Willie Marien, the accountant who had audited the Delorme books. He produced the same financial statements of the Delorme assets, revenues, and expenditures as those he had produced at the first trial and spent the day tediously explaining them to the jury. He told the court that the accused had regularly covered his deficits with Raoul's surplus.

During the afternoon recess, there was talk of prolonging the sessions until midnight in view of the trial's length and the intense heat which became insufferable during the afternoon sessions. The cool evening hours would make things more comfortable for everyone and would also expedite the trial, whose anticipated duration of two to three weeks had practically doubled because of the required translation.

Next morning, Calder produced Raoul's will and called Monsignor Rhéaume, former rector of the University of Ottawa and now bishop of Haileybury, Ontario. As the bishop approached the witness box, Judge Lemieux waived him away from it and graciously invited him to testify from the lawyers' bar. The bishop repeated the testimony he had given a year earlier. He told the court that on entering Raoul's hospital room he had seen the accused sitting on the corner of Raoul's bed and "the two brothers could be heard discussing the proposed

---

* Official translators are appointed by the Court (with the consent of counsel). They normally stand next to the witness simultaneously translating the questions and answers into the appropriate language for the benefit of the witness and the jury. A recent highly visible example of this (March 1995) was the English to Spanish translation for the testimony of Rosa Lopez in the O.J. Simpson case. With the lawyer's address to the jury, translation is not normally done on a sentence by sentence basis but rather at such time as the lawyer feels it to be appropriate.

contents of the will." The bishop's self-assurance impressed the court. At the end of his testimony, the judge excused him with a flourish and walked down from the bench to shake his hand.

One of Raoul's classmates next testified that Raoul had visited him during the Christmas break to reimburse $5 he had owed him. The witness recalled that Raoul had sworn him to secrecy about the transaction. Raoul's money was apparently a sensitive point with the accused. The witness said that although Raoul seemed satisfied with his brother's management, he had told him they had argued about it from time to time. This testimony obviously disturbed Delorme, who reacted angrily to some of it and conferred with his lawyers several times.

Calder was sure that the murder had been committed at 190 St Hubert Street. It was common knowledge that the three Delorme girls had been out from nine o'clock until about 11:30 on the evening of 6 January and that the accused had been home for at least most of that time. Collectively, the girls had been rather vague on this at the coroner's inquest, but Adélard himself had confirmed it. However, if Adélard had lied about Raoul having said over the telephone that he would be home late and Raoul had actually returned before seven o'clock, Adélard could have murdered him then. Calder wanted to open up another possibility – that he had committed the murder in the afternoon. To do so he would have to establish that the girls were out of the house long enough for this to take place. This would be more difficult to do because it went against statements previously made by Adélard and his sisters.

Calder began Saturday morning's session by telling the court that he would be calling the three Delorme girls in succession. He requested that they be excluded from the courtroom during each other's testimony and that they be sequestered from each other and not communicate with the accused until they had all testified. His request was granted. He then called Florence to the stand. She testified at length about the now well known activities in the Delorme house on the afternoon and evening of the sixth, but did concede that she had been out for a good part of the afternoon, returning at 5:15. Calder was pleased to have estalished that.

Rosa Delorme, wearing a perfectly cut dark suit, then confidently entered the courtroom and made her way to the witness stand. In her brief appearances at the coroner's inquest and the first trial she had been almost totally silent, saying she couldn't remember what had happened on 6 January. This time she had a wealth of detailed information, telling the court what every member of the family had done that day, stressing that the accused had left the house several times in the afternoon and that she herself was out for a couple of hours from about 4:15. "On my way back home from Rondeau's I even saw him coming out of St Jacques Church." When asked if she tried to catch up to him, she replied, "No, I was on the other side of the street and my brother is a fast walker. Anyway, he had told my sisters and me not to speak to him on the street because it could hint at impropriety and be the cause of gossip among passers-by."

Her testimony perfectly corroborated the accused's. George Farah-Lajoie, who was in the audience, was stunned by such precision, to the point that he began wondering if she might somehow have been involved in the murder. However, as far as Calder was concerned, two of the three girls had now admitted that they had been out of the house for part of the afternoon.

A rather bewildered-looking Lilly then took the stand. The police claimed she had already told them she had also been out that afternoon. If Calder could get her to repeat that in front of the jury, it would clear the way for his afternoon murder theory. The defence was obviously nervous when she began testifying – Lilly's mental weakness made her totally unpredictable, despite the fact that she had been very well prepared. Calder began his questioning in a quiet tone by asking Lilly at what time Raoul had left the house and how he was dressed. Although she was vague about what he was wearing and remembered that he "had talked about not wearing his overshoes because they hurt his feet," she remembered him leaving around 2:30 because she had watched him "walk down the street like a gendarme." Suddenly changing tone and shifting into intense, rapid-fire questioning, Calder continued, "At what time did you go out that afternoon?"

"I didn't go out."

"Not at all?"

"No, I stayed in the boudoir and living room all of the time."

"Did you say the contrary to Detective Pigeon?"

"No."

"Do you swear you didn't tell Detective Pigeon that you went out at 4 o'clock that afternoon?"

"No. I told him that I had not gone out, that I had spent the whole afternoon at home."

"So until what time did you stay home?"

"I didn't go out at all, only that evening at 8:15 to go to the theatre with Rosa and Mr Davis."

When asked if the outing had been prearranged, Lilly answered that as far as she knew the tickets had not been purchased beforehand and that they had told Adélard about it only as they were leaving.

"Immediately before leaving?", asked Calder.

"Around seven o'clock."

"Was he in the house when you left?"

"I believe he was."

"At what time did you return from the theatre?"

"At 11:20."

"How do you know it was 11:20?"

"Because Rosa showed me her watch and it was 11:20; she told me it was 11:20."

Calder quickly saw this as an opportunity to get Lilly to contradict herself and perhaps lose her self-control. He was virtually certain she didn't know how to tell the time and had been prompted by Rosa. He pulled out his vest watch and showed it to her.

"What time is it right now?"

"I know the time, Sir."

Calder held his watch under her eyes, and asked her to tell him the time. Without hesitation, she replied that it was 11:15. The courtroom clock showed 10:40.

Calder then focused on the late night activities in the basement. Lilly had testified that about 11:30 she had gone into the kitchen and seen the accused come up from the basement, get some matches and paper, and go back down. At midnight she went down to the basement and asked Adélard to come up and replace a small screw in the oven door. At that point in her testimony Lilly became very emotional and began crying profusely. Calder continued pressing.

"You say it was then midnight?"

"He came up around midnight and it took about ten minutes to fix the oven."

"And then he went back down to the basement?"

"Yes."

"How do you know it was midnight?"

"Because I heard it ring."

"Did you go to bed?"

"At midnight my brother went down to the basement and I went into the living room where I turned on the record player."

"Between 11:00 and midnight, did you hear the engine of your brother's car?"

"I didn't hear anything."

"Where were you when the accused came up for some matches?"

"I was in the kitchen boiling water to prepare myself a lemon grog."

"How was he dressed?"

"He was wearing his duster and his cap."

"Was he dirty?"

"He was covered with white dust."

"After having listened to some music, what did you do?"

"I heard one o'clock ring. I went down and asked my brother, 'Aren't you going to bed? It's past one o'clock.'"

"What did he say?"

"'I'll come up right away.' and he followed me up."

"Did you go to bed?"

"I went upstairs and got undressed."

"Next morning, what time did you get up?"

"At nine o'clock."

"Did someone tell you then that Raoul had not slept at home?"

"No one said anything to me."

"At nine o'clock that morning, did you notice that Raoul was not there?"

"I saw his bed had not been slept in."

Having gotten Lilly to contradict her previous statement about time, Calder thought he would try again. He was determined to have her admit she had been out for part of the afternoon.

"Between the time of Raoul's death and the coroner's inquest, did any detective question you?"

"Detectives came in the afternoon."

"Did they come often?"

"Yes."

"Did they ask you any questions?"

"I don't remember."

"You don't remember if you were asked any questions about your brother's murder?"

"They came in the morning to get my brother to identify the body."

"I understand that, but did those detectives ask you any questions when they inquired about what happened on the Feast of the Epiphany?"

"Some of them."

"Did they ask you particularly at what time you had gone out on the afternoon of the sixth?"

"I told them that I had not gone out of the house."

"You swear that?"

"Yes."

"I'm obliged to warn you that you're under oath. Are you stating positively that you did not tell any detective that you'd gone out that afternoon?"

"I didn't go out."

"And you didn't tell any detective that you had left the house that afternoon?"

"I said nothing."

Although Calder hadn't yet gotten the answer he had been hoping for, he decided not to persist in his attempt, at least for the moment, and turned the witness over to Taschereau for cross-examination. The defence attorney asked Lilly if she had spoken with Raoul before he went out on the afternoon of 6 January.

"Did he say anything to you?"

"I asked him 'Are you going to be late for dinner?' and he replied 'I don't know but I'll telephone. Don't worry I have my key.' and he left."

"Are you positive you didn't go out that afternoon?"

"Yes, I didn't go out, only that evening."

"Please don't be embarrassed now, but tell me, were you not indisposed that day?"

"I was sick and told my sister 'I'm not going out until this evening.'"

"I don't have to ask you what sickness, do I?"

"And I don't have to tell you."

Taschereau gave Lilly an approving nod. He liked that answer. It showed that Lilly was gaining confidence and hadn't been too intimidated by all this, something the defence had been afraid of. He decided to continue and, step by step, led her through her testimony about what happened during the latter part of the evening after she, her sister, and David returned home at 11:20. He was careful to have her confirm the various times which had already been mentioned.

"Did you hear him [Adélard] work?"

"Certainly and I went to see him. I asked him, 'What are you doing? Aren't you coming up?' and he answered, 'See, the furnace is dead and I'm trying to light it up. As soon as I do, I'll come up,' and he came up almost right away."

Lilly was doing so well that Taschereau felt he could safely come back to her ability to tell the time. That was the only flaw in her testimony. If he could neutralize that contradiction, then the rest of her testimony would hold. He took his watch out and asked the fundamentals of the minute and hour hands by having her point to their position at given times. Lilly explained her household routine of doing certain chores at regular times, such as preparing lunch at 11:30. But she unfortunately added that in order to be accurate she had adopted a procedure which consisted of combining the chimes on the clocks with the position of the hands. Then Calder, almost pouncing on her, shoved his watch in front of her eyes and asked her

the time. Stunned by the sudden move, she lost some of her composure and nervously replied that it was 1:25 when in fact it was 12:35.
At this point the accused, who had been attentively following his
sister's testimony while supporting her with eye contact and sounds
of encouragement, lost control of himself and shouted to Taschereau
from the prisoner's box, "Why don't you explain that she has poor
eyesight?"

Her plight had drawn a rare expression of sympathy from Delorme,
who seemed to feel sorry for her as she stumbled through her answers.
He obviously wanted to come to her defence and when the prison
doctor stared at him sternly for having prompted the witness,
Delorme shouted at him, "Some people aren't as smart as others." By
this time, Calder had brought in a large clock with classic arab
numerals instead of the roman numerals on most of the timepieces
shown Lilly. He set it at 4:40 and asked her to tell him the time. She
answered correctly. Overall, considering her limited mental capacity
and Calder's aggressive approach, Lilly had come through the ordeal
quite well. The defence felt that the Crown had not really under-
mined her testimony about not having been out that afternoon.

Richard Davis, Rosa's boyfriend, was called to the stand. Ever since
some spectators had caught a glimpse of him at the coroner's inquest,
there had been rumours that he was a negro. His appearance on the
scene prompted Delorme to shout to the press reporters, "There's
your famous negro! Look, he's no more a negro than you or I."
Although his features were caucasian, Davis was dark skinned – hence
the confusion.

Davis calmly told the court about going to the theater with Rosa
and Lilly that evening. His story was the same as that which had
already been heard except that he said the outing had been prearranged. This was contrary to Lilly's testimony and when asked by
Calder, "Who was there when the arrangement was made?" Davis
answered, "Lilly and Rosa. Rosa asked me if I had any objection to
her bringing Lilly and I told her I had none – so Rosa agreed to get
the tickets the next day." Ovide Tassé, Florence's friend, followed and
said that while he was at Delorme's early that evening he saw the
accused pass through the hallway but couldn't confirm if he was on
his way out of the house. As to his version of the decision to go to
the movies, he said it had been taken before he got there. He also
said he telephoned twice between 7 and 7:30 that evening, to which
Calder asked, "Can you tell us what was said?"

"The first time I telephoned, I asked if Florence was there and was
told she had left or at least that's what I understood."

"Did you give your name?"

"Not the first time."

"The second time, who came to the phone?"

"It was the same voice."

"And what was the conversation?"

"Again, I asked for Miss Florence. I was then asked to identify myself and said it was Mr Tassé. The voice inquired 'Aren't you the person who called a few minutes ago?' to which I answered yes. He told me 'I'm sorry, I thought that it was someone who was calling for my brother Raoul.'"

"Did you mention Raoul's name the first time?"

"No."

"Did you ask for Florence by her name?"

"Yes, I asked for Florence Delorme."

"And then Florence came to the telephone?"

"Yes, the second time."

"Did you hear something in the background while the line was open?"

"I couldn't tell."

Calder was disappointed. He hadn't yet proven that Adélard and Raoul had been home alone on that fateful day. It was now 2:30 and the trial was adjourned until Monday to allow everyone some enjoyment of the weekend. That afternoon, the exhausted jury was taken for a bus ride around town, stopping for a full course meal. Sunday morning they were taken to Mass and followed that up with a picnic on the shores of Lac St Louis. Throughout all these activities they were closely watched by officials of the Sheriff's office.

On Monday morning, 25 June, Pierre Emile Lalime, one of the accused's tenants, took the stand. He lived on the ground floor of the adjoining residence. His bedroom was located at the back of the house and was separated from the garage by a thin partition. Calder asked him: "Can you hear the engine of Delorme's car from your room?"

"Yes, I can hear his engine roar when he starts it in his garage."

"Did you hear Delorme's engine during the night of the sixth to the seventh of January?"

"Yes."

"Did you hear it once or several times?"

"Once."

"At what time was this?"

"Around 10:45."

"Was it before or after you went to bed?"

"After."

"Did you hear anything else?"

"At one o'clock, I heard someone shaking the furnace under my bedroom."

"Do you always hear the sound of the furnace being shaken when being loaded with coal?"

"Yes."

Under cross-examination Lalime admitted that on Christmas Day he had complained to Delorme about the lack of heat in his apartment. Delorme had even come to see him to explain that he couldn't find his furnace stoker. All accounts corroborated the accused's statement that he had been in his basement the night of the sixth.

Lalime's wife corroborated his testimony but added something which was possibly important. She was fairly sure Delorme had taken his car out of the garage that night because she remembered saying to her husband, as she got into bed, "Where can Father Delorme be going at this time of the night? Maybe he's been called to a sick bed."

Calder kept up the momentum by calling Percy Akin to the stand. Also a tenant, Akin lived in another flat near the garage. He said that around eleven o'clock that evening he had heard what sounded like a car trying to enter or leave the garage. The next morning he had noticed tiremarks in the laneway. They were clear, showed the imprint of winter chains, and led to the Delorme garage door. Calder had no further questions.

As the afternoon wore on, the courtroom became suffocatingly hot and the spectators, wedged in like sardines, became fidgety as they rubbed elbows and used everything in sight to fan themselves. Everyone was getting impatient and Delorme's behaviour didn't help. He paced back and forth in the prisoner's dock, fanning himself with his newspaper or scribbling notes which he handed to his lawyers as he angrily whispered instructions. It was obvious they were becoming irritated by their client.

Dominique Pusie, the first detective to have seen the body in Snowdon, was the next witness. To everyone's surprise, he began his testimony by producing Delorme's broken watch chain. Embarrassed, he told the court he had removed it from Raoul's vest at the morgue and had found it the evening before his testimony, wedged between the pages of his notebook. He hadn't mentioned it before because he had thought he had lost it. It was now certain that the watch had been ripped off Raoul's vest.

Visibly upset, defence counsel's patience reached its limit when Delorme, who hadn't let up on his bizarre behaviour, interrupted Pusie's testimony by giving him an exaggerated military salute and mocking smile. The judge decided to adjourn for fifteen minutes to air the room.

When the hearing resumed, Calder asked for a further adjournment until the next day. Utterly exhausted by the demands of the trial and the sleepless nights required to prepare his case, he said he just couldn't go on. The judge granted his request.

The next day Oscar Haynes, the gunsmith, told about the accused's visit to his shop on 27 December. The accused had come for repairs to his Iver Johnson but at the gunsmith's suggestion had decided to exchange it for a new Bayard, an automatic, modern, rapidfire revolver. At the same time he had bought two boxes of bullets, some oil, a brush, and some grease.

"Before giving him the weapon, did you give him some instruction?" asked Calder

"Yes, I gave all the necessary instructions."

"Did you talk about testing the weapon after the sale?"

"Yes."

"At your suggestion?"

"Yes, I have a target range."

"Did you fire at the target?"

"Yes."

"Did the priest fire at the target?"

"Yes."

"How many times did you fire?"

"I fired about 4 times."

"Did you fire to show the rapid motion of the pistol?"

"That's exactly what I was doing."

"How many bullets does the magazine hold?"

"Six."

"You fired four shots and then you stopped?"

"That was the number of bullets I had put in the gun."

The judge asked how many times the accused had fired the pistol. Haynes said he remembered him having fired three or four times. He said that the bullets used were those of the priest and that after they had done the firing he had thoroughly cleaned the gun before giving it to Delorme.

Next came a lengthy and technical testimony by Dr Wilfrid Derome who, with the help of the mannequin that had been so controversial a year earlier, explained the trajectory of the bullets in the victim's body. Raoul's bloodstained shirt was produced, as were his shoes. The judge asked Derome if the shoes were wet when the body was brought to the morgue. "No, they were dry and the nail heads in the soles were shiny. I examined them on the morning the body was discovered," he answered.

He had found seven bullet wounds in the victim's head and neck, but had found only two bullets during the autopsy. Derome felt that there might still be some bullets in the body. With the help of a drawing, he showed the jury how he thought they had been fired. The first, which showed powder marks, had been shot at extremely close range and had entered about one inch above the right ear. The second, which had entered halfway between the mouth and the jaw, had been shot from a bit further out. The third, fourth, and fifth holes were in the lower part of the head, the last one having apparently entered the right side of Raoul's head slightly under the jaw, pieced clearly through his neck and continued its path through his collar. This one, he said, "made two holes and explains the extra or seventh wound." Cahan interrupted: "Wouldn't it be possible for two persons to have fired those bullets?"

"As far as I'm concerned, it's highly improbable but not impossible."

"I'm not asking your opinion, I'm simply asking if it was possible?"

"And I'm saying that it's not impossible to imagine that."

"And it's certain, isn't it, that if all six or seven shots had been fired by a single person, that person would have alternatively been standing on one side of the victim and then on his other side?"

"Exactly."

The following day Calder announced that, as a result of Dr Derome's testimony, Raoul's body would be exhumed for a second autopsy. On hearing this, the accused was visibly shaken. He flinched and trembled for a few moments as he looked around the courtroom with an expression of concern. Sir François Lemieux called him to order and instructed the Crown to proceed with its next witness.

George Joseph Woods, a mechanic for the Canadian Pacific Railway, testified that sometime between 11:30 and midnight on 6 January, while walking home from work, he had noticed a car stopped by the curb on the east side of Décarie Boulevard on the edge of a vacant field between Western Avenue (now de Maisonneuve) and Sherbrooke. A broad shouldered man of about 5 feet 8 inches tall wearing a racoon coat and fur hat was standing at the right rear side of the car. Thinking he had mechanical problems, Woods approached the man but quickly got the impression his help wasn't needed. He returned to the opposite sidewalk and continued on his way home. By the time he got to Sherbrooke Street, the car was heading north. It was too dark for him to identify the person. He did say, however, that the shape of the car was similar to the accused's, which he had examined earlier at the municipal garage.

The next day's proceedings got under way in an atmosphere of heated and violent debate: Farah-Lajoie was taking the stand. Defence counsel strongly objected to his testifying and asked for a *voir dire*,* claiming he was a bigoted, anti-clerical atheist who attached absolutely no value to the oath. According to the defence, his book, *Ma version de l'affaire Delorme*, concluded that Delorme was guilty, automatically disqualifying him as a witness. With the jury excused, Farah-Lajoie was rigorously questioned. It was clear that Taschereau would do his best to have the detective cited for contempt of court. The *Toronto Globe* of 29 June reported that "defence counsel Taschereau accused Lajoie of having written a book of ignominious accusations against Abbé Delorme."

"Did you not at one time tell your colleagues that you didn't believe in God and that the only religion was that which produced the greatest pleasure with the greatest number of women, namely that of Mohamed?"

"No. I deny it categorically; I always believed in God, I believe in him now, and will do so all my life."

After a lengthy debate, against the background of a stream of groans, exaggerated facial twitches and body shakes coming from the accused, Judge Lemieux ruled that Farah-Lajoie could testify but admonished him for the bias he had shown in his book.

Before Farah-Lajoie took the stand, a clerk brought out an elaborate wooden model of the Delorme house. Built by Dr Derome, it could be separated into several sections and showed the floor plan of the Delorme house, from the basement to the top floor, in great detail. With the help of the model, the detective told of his first visit on St Hubert Street, stressing the priest's sarcastic reaction to his suicide theory. "He thought I was rather stupid to think that someone could shoot six bullets into himself." Something bothered Calder about Farah-Lajoie's testimony – he couldn't put his finger on it, but a couple of pieces didn't seem to fit. Detectives Pigeon and Desgroseillers and Chief Lorrain followed Farah-Lajoie to the stand. Pigeon revealed that on one of his visits he had found another quilt, this time in a suitcase which belonged to Lilly. It too, he said, matched the quilt found on Raoul's body. Desgroselliers told the jury

---

* Literally, to speak the truth. A preliminary examination by the court, without the presence of the jury, of a person presented as a witness or a juror where his or her competency or interest is objected to.

about seeing Raoul's freshly laundered bedsheets hanging in the stairwell on the morning of 7 January 1922. Lorrain told about receiving the accused's watch. He was convinced that Delorme himself had mailed it. Indeed, after he received the watch, he had spoken about it to only three people – the assistant attorney general, Crown Prosecutor Walsh, and a police detective responsible for the custody of trial exhibits. "It was highly unlikely," he said, "that any of them would have passed that information on to Delorme. Yet a few hours later a reporter spoke to me about it at Delorme's request. I found that odd."

While the courtroom activities took up center stage, there was a lot going on behind the scenes. Much of it revolved around legal fees. Having been civilly interdicted, Delorme did not have access to his money. At the start of the trial Cahan had requested an advance of $5,000 from Delorme's curator. On Gustave Monette's advice, the curator refused. Monette was still the curator's lawyer and, by extension, Delorme's, at least, from the civil point of view, regarding his capacity to act. Tétreault and Monette were still convinced that the insanity plea was the best defence for their ward and felt that an advance against defence counsel's fees might jeopardize their right to challenge the defence's strategy later. Monette wrote Cahan, criticizing him for having waited so long to ask for funds. His letter also insisted that Cahan had been hired by Delorme without the curator's consent, and that the curator hadn't been consulted regarding Delorme's defence. Cahan was upset. He replied that he was not requesting anything for his services but that the $5,000 was for handwriting expertise, biological tests, and investigation costs.

We were not sure until the opening of the trial, and until the Chief Justice had denied the application to place the defence of Abbé Delorme in your control, that we would be permitted to act as his counsel at this trial. Therefore we were not in the position, prior to that date, to ask you as curator to advance funds for his defence. So far, we have paid all expenses out of our own funds; therefore the responsibility of seeing an innocent man go to the scaffold for lack of funds to present his defence properly before the court now rests upon you.

The defence was eventually promised an advance. However, there was now only $300 cash in the estate. The curator would have to borrow the balance and mortgage Delorme's properties, a lengthy process. So the curator suggested that Cahan obtain an advance from the Crown. Cahan immediately began this procedure.

In court, on 29 June Dr McTaggart was called to provide details of the second autopsy, which had revealed a third bullet lodged in the neck. The exhumed skull and bullet were closely examined by the jury. Calder asked Dr MacTaggart:

"Doctor, could you tell us how you found the third bullet?"

"I examined the body; its skin was still stuck to the bones in such a way that the bullet holes near the ear and chin were still very visible."

"With the help of your drawing of the wounds, could you tell us which bullets you were searching for?"

"I was looking for the bullet identified with the opening marked "A" on the drawing at one inch from the earlobe. When we examined the head, we noticed the skin was intact on that side and we could therefore track the bullet hole in the skin. It was the same thing for each bullet hole. By lifting the skin on the face, the upper jaw appeared and we could easily see the penetrating wound."

"Could you easily see the upper part of the jaw?"

"Yes."

"Does the wound marked "A" on your drawing continue into the bone?"

"Yes, and by penetrating into the bone it pushed part of it inward."

"Would the penetration of the bone slow down the bullet's path?"

"Yes, this slowed down the bullet. On examination we noticed that this bullet did not reach the brain or the opposite jaw."

"Did you try to pass a prober through to follow the bullet's path?"

"We couldn't do that because of the condition of the head; there were too many larvae."

"Had the tissues inside the head disappeared?"

"Yes, and it was easy to see if that bullet had reached the superior part of the brain or the opposite jaw. We then proceeded to a careful examination of the neck; the skin had disappeared and the spinal cord was exposed. Dr Derome lifted the left tissue, applied a great deal of pressure, and we found a hard substance."

"What was that substance?"

"A bullet."

The bullet was produced and examined by the judge and jury. Pointing to Raoul's skull, Calder continued:

"Doctor, is this bullet of the same calibre as those found in the first autopsy?"

"To the naked eye, it appears to be the same."

"Would you introduce the bullet into the jaw and tell us if it easily enters the wound?"

The doctor complied. "It does," he said. "The hole is slightly larger and the bullet easily fits in."

"Is that what normally happens?"

"Yes, the hole is always slightly larger than the diameter of the bullet."

"Could you tell us where the jaw was fractured?"

"Yes, it is very visible, in the center."

"Did you examine below the eighth vertebrae to find the other bullet?"

"Yes, we searched right down to the bottom of the shoulder blade."

"Why wasn't the other bullet ever found?"

"As it went through the other cavity of the mouth it must have been spit out with small pieces of bone."

"Up to date, three bullets have been found?"

"Yes."

All eyes turned to the prisoner's box as Delorme, who had been watching the tests on his brothers skull in obvious agony, suddenly burst into tears and dropped his head out of sight below the prisoner's railing.

After MacTaggart's testimony, Haynes, the gunsmith, returned to the stand and testified that when he exchanged the Bayard it was properly oiled and greased. Later, when the police showed it to him, it showed more grease and oil than would have been used by someone experienced with guns. He explained the tests he made under the watchful eye of Farah-Lajoie. First he had fired a bullet from Delorme's Bayard, then another from his own Bayard, and finally a bullet from a Browning and a Mauser. He showed the jury that the bullets shot from both Bayards had the same grooves except for a distinctive scar on the Delorme bullet, which he explained had been caused by a flaw in the lining of the barrel.

Calder showed him the three bullets taken from Raoul's body. Haynes examined them with a magnifying glass and concluded that they had been fired from Delorme's Bayard: the telltale scars on all three of them proved it.

The defence was disturbed by Haynes' testimony. It had no one available who could refute it and complained to the court about not having the Crown's means to secure an expert witness. The defence had not given much attention to possible evidence from ballistics, but now realized that it could be important and requested a delay to find an expert. It was granted.

Dr Derome returned to the witness box. Although his expertise was internationally recognized in forensic medicine, the Crown had to establish it regarding ballistics. It did so by having him describe a technique he had learned in Paris. Known as "bullet rolling," it consisted of rolling a bullet on either carbon or zinc paper. A bright light was then projected on the paper and it was photographed. The result was a clear picture of the bullet, highlighting its grooves and scars. Calder asked him: "On the basis of your experiment, is it your opinion that bullet P-48, fired with Delorme's Bayard, and bullet exhibits P-20 , P-26b, and P-57, taken from the deceased's body, were fired from the same weapon?

"Yes, sir."

It was apparent that the bullet fired from Haynes' Bayard did not have the same characteristics as that fired from Delorme's. The bullets were closely examined by each member of the jury and Derome carefully explained the grooves and distinctive scratches caused by a defect in the revolutions of the bullet as it passed through the barrel. With the help of a large wooden model he had built of a bullet travelling through a gun barrel, he gave the jury a brief demonstration. When asked what might have happened to the three other bullets, Derome replied that they had gone through Raoul's body and in doing so lost their force and simply fell next to the body.

His testimony created a great deal of interest. Although ballistics had already been used as evidence in European trials, this was probably the first time it had been used to such an extent in North America.* All the talk about the bullets suddenly reminded Calder of what had bothered him in Farah-Lajoie's testimony and he planned to come back to it.

Derome was also cross-examined about his testimony regarding the blood found in Delorme's car and admitted that the scientific techniques used in blood identification could sometimes be fallible. Before the witness stepped down, Calder surprisingly asked if he could re-examine. Cahan had no objection.

"When did you first disclose that six bullets had been fired into Raoul's body?"

---

* In 1860 a murderer in England was tracked down because of the accidental identification of bullet grooves with those in the barrel of his revolver. However, because the identification was considered to be accidental, there was no follow-up on this method. Some thirty years later in Lyon, France, professor Alexandre Lacassagne of the *Faculté de Médecine de Lyon* assisted at a murder investigation by analysing bullet grooves in relation to the weapon from which they were fired. In 1915, in upstate New York, a convicted murderer was pardoned when it was shown that the murder bullets had not been fired from his revolver. An unsatisfactory attempt at bullet comparison was also made in the famous 1921 trials of Sacco and Vanzetti in the United States.

"At the preliminary hearing in March 1922."

"Who else knew about it?"

"Dr MacTaggart, who performed the autopsy with me."

"Did any one but the two of you know about the six bullets?"

"Not as far as I know."

Calder excused Derome and recalled Farah-Lajoie to the stand.

"Would you repeat what the accused said to you when you suggested the possibility of a suicide?

"He said 'That's ridiculous. How could someone fire six bullets into his head?'"

"When did he say that to you?"

"The first day I met him, 9 January 1922."

The answer caused quite a stir in the courtroom.

The Crown then showed the proposed route from the Delorme home to Snowdon by way of Decarie Boulevard and back via St Michel Street, which would take about an hour to drive.

The trial was beginning its thirteenth day. This was a record for the Montreal Criminal Assizes, passing the twelve-day insanity hearing in the same case a year earlier. The Crown called on Charles Hazen, an American handwriting expert. As with ballistics, there was much controversy at that time over the value of handwriting analysis as evidence. After having compared the handwriting on the box addressed to Chief Lorrain with the handwriting on several cheques, promissory notes, and receipts signed by Delorme, Hazen concluded that Delorme had written the address, stating, "There are fifteen characteristics of the accused which appear in the small amount of writing on the box. If there had been one or even two similarities, it could pass for a coincidence. As it is, I have no doubt that the writing is by the same person."

Hazen's opinion was corroborated by J.J. Lomax, who added that the odds of two adults having the same handwriting were about 64 trillion to one. He considered handwriting identification as reliable as fingerprinting. Lomax was a convincing witness. Cahan decided to try to discredit him by challenging his qualifications. That backfired when he was reminded that he himself had retained Lomax as a handwriting expert on two previous occasions.

The most prestigious expert was Albert S. Osborne* of New York, whose official letterhead described him as "Examiner of Questioned Documents." Of international repute, he had written many texts on handwriting and had figured in many important trials both in Canada and the United States. Quebec ecclesiastical authorities had even used his services to identify scriptural writings. After a lengthy demonstration, Osborne came to the same conclusion as his two colleagues: "To the best of my knowledge, these writings were made by the same person."

After the noon recess, Jules Goyer, one of the jurors, was granted permission to address the court. The heat wave, which made the unventilated courtroom unbearable, and the tedious testimony of handwriting experts were starting to tell on the jury. Goyer made a formal request that the Crown speed up its case. He said many of the jury members were in a state of depression at having been away from their families and occupations for so long and, considering that the defence had not yet presented its case, he asked the Crown to shorten its expert testimony. Crown prosecutor Calder replied that he would do his best, but emphasized that the defence's extensive cross-examination of the Crown's witnesses was equally responsible and that the defence's choice of a bilingual jury required simultaneous translation, which doubled the length of each testimony. The defence counsel attempted to reassure the jury by stating that presentation of its case would not take more than five days. He also seized the opportunity to ask that the court request the Crown to finance the expert testimony required by the defence, which it would otherwise be unable to afford and which was required to challenge the Crown.

The next witnesses were brief. A cobbler said that the shoes found on Raoul's body had never been worn outdoors, and a salesman with Légaré Automobile, the Montreal distributor which had sold Delorme his Franklin, testified that in 1922 there were only 200 such cars in the city, that it could reach a speed of 45 m.p.h., and that its distinctive shape made it stand out. Someone from the McGill Observatory testified that a mixture of frozen rain and snow covered the roads on 5 January 1922 and froze hard on the day of the sixth as the temperature dropped by about 30° fahrenheit. By the night of the sixth, road surfaces had become hard and irregular. A car mechanic then testified that on the morning of 7 January Delorme brought his Franklin to his garage to have a new set of chains installed on the rear tires and some broken links replaced on the front ones. The Crown suggested

---

* Ten years later Osborne would play an important role in sending Bruno Richard Hauptmann to the electric chair for the kidnapping and murder of Charles Lindbergh's baby. It was his testimony that identified the infamous ransom notes as having been written by Hauptmann.

that he had damaged the previous pair during his drive through the city with Raoul's body on the preceding night.

Feeling somewhat more confident, Calder decided, over defence counsel's objections, to recall Lilly.

"Did you not, on 9 January, tell Detective Pigeon, in the presence of Detectives Farah-Lajoie and Desgroseillers, that you went out at 4 o'clock on the sixth?" Lilly categorically denied this. Pigeon then took the stand and swore to the contrary – just as categorically – adding that she had repeated her statement to Chief Lepage in his office after the first session of the coroner's inquest. Calder decided not to take this line of questioning any further. For the time being he would rely on the suspicion created by the policeman's testimony, especially when Pigeon reminded the court that, during one of the first visits to the Delorme home, the accused had remarked, "You can see there's a window in the basement. We can be seen from outside and people would have heard if someone had been shot here, so isn't that proof that nothing happened here?" Pigeon told the jury he wondered why Delorme had said that, "considering that he wasn't under any suspicion at the time, nor had there been any suggestion that his home was the scene of the crime." He said neither he nor Farah-Lajoie had suspected Delorme until a week later when they found out about the gun.

Wednesday, 11 July, marked the trial's third week. Calder moved to introduce Delorme's deposition at the coroner's inquest as evidence. Taschereau objected. He reminded the court that because Delorme was obligated to testify at the coroner's inquest, he was entitled to protection in that his testimony could not be used against him. However, now he was on trial and therefore not a compellable witness. Producing his deposition would in effect be forcing the accused to testify against his wishes, which was against a fundamental rule of law. Judge Lemieux unhesitatingly agreed and sustained the objection.

Calder had bad news for Cahan next morning. The attorney general's office had turned down the defence's request for funds. Frustrated and disappointed, Cahan asked for his expert witnesses to be summoned at the expense of the Crown. Judge Lemieux told him the court had no such authority and Calder added that the Crown couldn't possibly remunerate a witness whose purpose was to discredit the Crown's own experts. As a last resort, Cahan requested that the proceedings be suspended until funds could be found. His request was denied.

That afternoon the court moved to 190 St Hubert, where a large crowd of bystanders watched as the judge, jury, and lawyers were given a thorough tour of the Delorme house. The Delorme girls were fascinated by the sight of the judge and his entourage of about sixty people, who arrived in a motorcade of fifteen cars followed by twelve motorcycled policemen. Rosa greeted them at the door and accompanied the group as it was taken through every nook and cranny. The accused looked at each room affectionately, a man returning home after an eighteen-month absence. The unusual procession prompted Lilly to quip, "There are more people than for the St Jean Baptiste Parade." On leaving the house Delorme saluted some of his neighbours, who were milling about, and the procession moved on, following the route alleged to have been taken the night of the crime. It formed an impressive caravan as it made its way to Décarie Boulevard, up to the Snowdon junction, northeast towards St Michel, and back downtown to St Hubert street. It stopped at several locations along the route to allow for the comments of some of the witnesses.

A front page story of the 13 July *Toronto Globe* reported that the bus carrying the jury had crashed into Judge Lemieux's car on the way from Delorme's house to Décarie boulevard, where Wood showed them the site of the car he noticed on the night of 6 January. The story went on to state that "some damage was done to his lordship's car. The jury seemed to be more frightened than the chief justice."

The court ended its outing at the municipal garage where it examined the Franklin, which had been impounded more than a year earlier. Delorme accompanied the court throughout its journey but didn't show much interest until they reached the garage. He then came to life, got into his car, and began enthusiastically explaining its finer points until his lawyer stopped him.

The Crown had all but concluded its case. However Calder wanted to make one last attempt to get Lilly to change her testimony. The next morning he called on Chief Lepage, who told the court that on 9 January, after the first session of the coroner's inquest, he had invited Adélard and his sisters into his office to extend his condolences. He said that in the course of the conversation Lilly had told him she had gone out on the afternoon of 6 January around four o'clock and had returned at supper time. Calder settled for that. He would have preferred Lilly's own acknowledgment that she had been out, but felt that he had put enough contradictory evidence in the record to undermine her testimony. Having her take the stand again after Lepage's testimony might only confuse things and antagonize the jury.

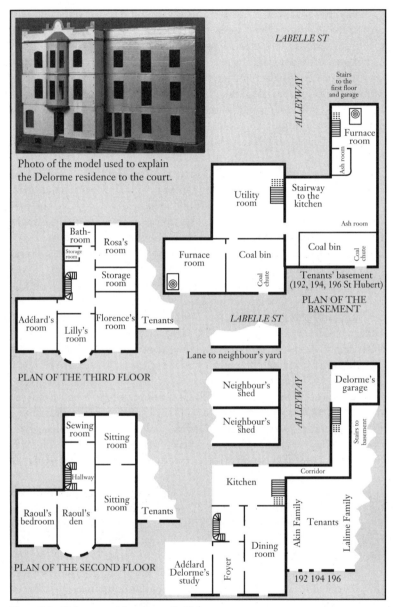

Photo of the model used to explain the Delorme residence to the court.

LABELLE ST

ALLEYWAY

Stairs to the first floor and garage

Furnace room

Ash room

Utility room

Stairway to the kitchen

Ash room

Furnace room

Coal bin

Coal chute

Coal bin

Coal chute

Tenants' basement (192, 194, 196 St Hubert)

PLAN OF THE BASEMENT

Bath-room

Storage room

Rosa's room

Storage room

Adélard's room

Lilly's room

Florence's room

Tenants

PLAN OF THE THIRD FLOOR

LABELLE ST

Lane to neighbour's yard

Neighbour's shed

Delorme's garage

ALLEYWAY

Sewing room

Sitting room

Neighbour's shed

Stairs to basement

Hallway

Sitting room

Corridor

Kitchen

Raoul's bedroom

Raoul's den

Tenants

Akin Family

Tenants

Lalime Family

PLAN OF THE SECOND FLOOR

Adélard Delorme's study

Foyer

Dining room

192 194 196

Plan of the Delorme residence, 190 St Hubert.

The Crown rested its case. Calder thought he had done his best although he knew there were still missing pieces and unanswered questions. Were the Delorme sisters involved? What did they know? What about Leclerc, the furnace-stoker? He might have been able to fit some pieces into the puzzle but he had left Montreal a couple of months before the trial and couldn't be located. It was rumoured that he had fled to the United States. Despite all of these missing links, Calder was confident he could obtain a conviction.

The defence began by drawing attention to the story of Michael Barry, the ship chandler, about apparent criminal activity in the harbour area in the early morning hours of 7 January. Barry told the jury that as he was crossing Place d'Armes on St Sulpice Street on his way home from a late card game he saw someone trying to remove a large object from a car stopped along the river wall on rue De La Commune. On noticing Barry, the man pushed the object back in the car which then proceeded up the street while the man stood on the running board with a gun in his hand. "St Sulpice is a one-way street leading south, but the car was coming north towards Notre Dame," added Barry. "It stopped near my shop just below St Paul street. I hesitated to walk on, thinking they might hold me up, but I saw that wasn't the case when the car turned west on St Paul. There was a slight hill there and they couldn't drive over it, so they backed up and continued on St Sulpice. I hid behind a telephone pole and prepared for an attack, but the car sped by and disappeared in the distance."

According to Barry, the car looked like a McLaughlin and had three occupants and a bulky white bundle in the back seat. "I didn't pay much attention to it at the moment because it is not unusual to see suspicious activities in that district."

Oscar Nolet testified that he had seen a McLaughlin heading west on St Catherine Street at about the same time with two men in the front seat and what looked like a body wrapped in a blanket in the back seat, its arm dangling out the window as far down as the mud guard.

The Crown prosecutor was somewhat surprised at the defence's line of evidence. If anything, Calder felt it might help his case. A driver leaving the harbour area and heading for Snowdon would normally take St Catherine west and then go north on Décarie, where Woods had also seen a car at about that time. As to the make of the car, both witnesses could have been mistaken.

The defence tried to get corroboration from the neighbours of Delorme's testimony about his comings and goings on the day of the sixth. Various of his tenants said that he was in the basement between eleven o'clock and midnight.

Leclerc's landlord said Delorme came to get Leclerc around five o'clock on the afternoon of the sixth and that Leclerc had come home at about nine o'clock.

The defence then called a series of witnesses to explain the blood-stains found in Delorme's car. One of them told the court that Delorme had taken him and his eight-year-old son for a drive to the Trappist Monastery at Oka, some forty miles from Montreal, and that the boy had a nosebleed in the back seat. The witness's testimony became blatantly suspect when under cross-examination he couldn't remember the date of the trip, the road they had taken, the names of any villages they had gone through, or the number of rivers they had crossed. "You went to Oka in November of 1921, you remember your son's nosebleed, but you don't remember anything else about the trip," Calder said sarcastically. The witness answered that his son was being treated by a doctor for chronic nosebleeds. He was further discredited when he couldn't remember the doctor's name and said he had just died. Instead of dropping what appeared to be a weak line of evidence, the defence persisted. Fedora Vincent testified that his eight-year-old daughter Marguerite had also had a nosebleed in the Franklin on New Year's Eve, a week before the murder. Vincent said that he and his wife, Rita, who were good friends of Delorme, had invited him over on the evening of 6 January but he had declined. Another explanation about the blood stains was furnished by Eugène Delorme, the accused's first cousin. He said that in October 1921, the accused, who had driven to St Scholastic to officiate at a family wedding, invited him to hop in for a drive. He accepted the invitation but as he got in the car he cut his hand on the door. While riding, he handled some cushions on back seat and some blood dripped onto them.

Calder didn't bother to cross-examine. Under normal circumstances, these testimonies might have been credible, but he felt he had so discredited the first witness that he could let the overly coincidental nature of the other stories speak for themselves. Marguerite herself was led to the witness stand and described how she had bled all over Delorme's three car cushions. Farah-Lajoie shook his head in disbelief as he leaned over and reminded Calder that the accused had said that the blood was his own, from a finger he cut while working on the car.

George Albert Field, a handwriting expert for the defence, testified that the forger was a person with little education who had simply copied a handwritten letter by Delorme that had been reproduced in a newspaper. Some of the letters, particularly the capital *D*, were unlike Delorme's and gave away the forgery. Calder observed, "Your statement is that this comparatively uneducated man reasoned as follows: 'I want to forge the Abbé's handwriting; consequently I will make my capital *D* as unlike his as possible.'"

The next morning, however, the defence's case improved. Alleyn Taschereau told the court that he had always been convinced that the murder had been committed in Côte Saint Michel, an area of the city well known for its night clubs and active nightlife. "Following that hunch, we did some investigating and last night, at the eleventh hour, we found two witnesses who saw Raoul and clearly recognized him late in the evening of 6 January. The court has my word that I would have produced these witnesses earlier if I had found them before. Both have been silent until now because they didn't want to be exposed to criticism. However, now that they realize that a man's life is in danger, they have consented to come here this morning and offer their testimony to the court."

The first of these men, Charles Edward Globensky, took the stand. Manager of a private club (the Olympic), he testified that at about 11:30 on the night of 6 January four men drove up to the club but he turned them away because they were not members. He was sure one of them was Raoul Delorme. He remembered the incident quite well because it had been a quiet night at the club and theirs was only the second car he had seen all evening.

Calder didn't believe Globensky. He had been told that the detectives had visited the witness shortly after the murder and that at that time he had claimed never to have seen Raoul. Under rather stiff cross-examination, the witness stuck to his story, adding, "Someone else will come to testify about that later on." Calder pounced on him:

"And you know what he's going to say? How do you know?"

"Well, it's because after ...'

"Because you spoke with him last night?"

"Well, we work together."

"Did you speak about this case last night?"

"Not really, but he told me after the lawyers left last night, 'It's him all right, I recognize him.'"

Calder must have unnerved Globensky who, after that exchange, became increasingly vague. He failed to remember how Raoul was dressed, his size, the size of his companions, or who else came to the club that evening. He did remember, however, that Raoul was wearing eyeglasses and a pale cap – information he could have read in the newspaper.

The other surprise witness was Lorenzo Roy. An employee of the Tremblay Hotel, adjacent to the Olympic Club, Roy had been working the parking lot that evening and turned back four men who had driven up in a large McLaughlin. Roy was later visited by the police and he identified Raoul's photograph as showing one of the people he had seen in that car, "I told him it looked very much like the person I had seen in the car, but I couldn't swear to it."

If true, Globensky and Roy's testimony would provide evidence that someone other than the accused could have been the murderer. However, they lacked credibility. As last-minute witnesses, their testimony had probably been inspired by what they had read in the newspapers, particularly the late-night sighting of a McLaughlin racing around the city by Barry and Nolet.

Despite its lack of funds, the defence, at long last, had found a ballistics expert. William Jones had been a firearms expert for the New York City police for twenty years. He testified that the bullets that killed Raoul had been fired from two guns. He produced a Bayard bearing serial number 34678, one digit below the number of Delorme's handgun, and explained that bullets fired from two guns carrying consecutive serial numbers could easily have the same marks, because the same rifling tools would have been used. He demonstrated how he had made comparisons with the help of another expert, Albert Hamilton. They had concluded that "It would be impossible to produce a good imprint by rolling the bullets on zinc paper. Given the shape of these two bullets, I don't know how this could have been done." On hearing Hamilton's name, Calder remembered that a man named Hamilton had been involved in the conviction and death sentence of a farmhand in a 1915 New York murder trial. At that trial Hamilton had testified that the bullets removed from the victim's body had been fired out of a handgun belonging to the farmhand. After the trial, his testimony was challenged and the governor of New York ordered an investigation. Hamilton's testimony was rejected and his so-called expert demonstrations to the jury were exposed as no more than trickery. The person who had carried out the first, and discredited, investigation was none other than William Jones, then a captain in the New York police force. On learning that Hamilton was in the courtroom, Calder jumped to his feet and interrupted the witness: "I demand that this man be removed from the room and I want to know where that other Bayard came from." An angry Taschereau replied, "You will find out when Mr Hamilton testifies and not before. Furthermore, there is absolutely no reason why he should be removed from the courtroom." That was precisely the reaction Calder was hoping for. "I will tell you the reason," he replied forcefully. "Mr Hamilton is a dangerous witness. Mr Hamilton is known all over the United States as a fabricator of evidence. I insist that he be removed."

With an imperious gesture, the judge pointed to the door and ordered, "Get him out." A guard escorted Hamilton from the room. A furious Cahan told the court that Jones had examined the bullets in his own apartment in the presence of a detective and without Hamilton.

Calder still didn't trust the results of anything Hamilton had been associated with. His cross-examination revealed that Hamilton had played an important part in the tests and the preparation of the evidence. As the questioning wore on, Hamilton's role started to embarrass the defence. The Crown was showing that one of its experts, who had handled the bullets and made the drawings used in the evidence, had previously been involved in fabricating evidence. At one point Jones disassociated himself from Hamilton by admitting to Calder that he would never have recommended him to the defence. Calder even got Jones to admit that someone with a knowledge of firearms could mount a revolver on a lathe and, through a slight pressure to one side, create an imperfect trajectory which would duplicate the unusual scar on the bullets found in Raoul's body. Defence counsel now moved to prevent Hamilton's notoriety from tainting their own reputations. Cahan rose and asked the witness:

"Mr. Jones, I wish to clarify one or two facts. The first time I spoke to you over the phone was on 30 June, was it not?"

"Yes."

"And did I not follow that up with a letter written on 2 July?"

"Yes."

"And then, after an exchange of correspondence, did I not ask you to be available on short notice?"

"Yes. I received that letter last Thursday."

"In my instructions to you, did I not say that I wanted the facts and if the facts were against Abbé Delorme, I would not stand in the way of his going to the scaffold?"

"Yes, you mentioned that on the telephone and you repeated it in your apartment."

Cahan then addressed the bench. "I do not wish to inject my personality into this. I was brought up in the fear of God and I have lived this life so that I can look any man in the face and tell him to go to Hell, if necessary. My reputation will stand apart from what any detective or any other man says." No one was interested in questioning Jones further. He was excused from the witness stand and the hearing was adjourned for the day. Delorme's lawyers were visibly upset. Testimony they had hoped would weaken the Crown's case had instead forced them to reject their own witness.

Hints that the defence was fabricating evidence continued after the adjournment. An incensed Taschereau was as vocal as Cahan in resenting this. Calder quickly replied, "I'm not insinuating anything against my learned friends. To the contrary, I believe that a case has never been conducted with more integrity. But we can all be duped. Here's a man called Hamilton, who professes to be the source of all the secrets of science, who calls himself an expert and is ready to tell the other experts how to do things, regardless of their opinions. I know everything I need to know about this man's character. I'm suggesting that my learned friends didn't know his character, that they have been duped. This morning their own witness said he wouldn't recommend Hamilton. I know him by reputation and I thought that I should warn the court in the interest of truth and justice." Next morning the defence again insisted that it had never been its intention to fabricate evidence. "We did our best to get experts," said a dejected Taschereau, "and the only one we could come up with was Mr Jones."

Rosa Delorme returned to the stand to clarify certain things, particularly Raoul's will. She had overheard the accused tell Raoul, "Give according to your heart," during a telephone conversation between the priest and his brother on 5 February 1921, a few days before Raoul's operation. Taschereau also felt an explanation was in order concerning Raoul's bedsheets, which had been hanging up to dry on the morning of 7 January. "Wasn't that unusual," Taschereau asked, "considering that Raoul hadn't slept there the night before?" Rosa replied that Lilly usually did the laundry on Wednesdays and Saturdays. The seventh was a Saturday and she knew Raoul would be leaving for Ottawa. It was normal for Lilly to launder his sheets.

To add weight to his theory that the murder had been committed in Côte St Michel, Taschereau called on Yvonne Constantineau, who, on the evening of 6 January had been working at her father's drug store near the Olympic Club. She testified that Raoul came to the store between seven and eight o'clock that evening. "He wanted to buy some aspirin. I remember him because he paid with a $5 gold coin and I had to go up to my father's apartment for change. I never thought of telling anyone until Mr Taschereau's recent visit." Her uncle, a lawyer, who had been visiting her family at the time and had witnessed the incident, added that "a few days ago, while in the court-house corridor chatting about the Delorme case, I brought up the incident of my niece and the $5 gold coin. A few minutes later Mr Cahan came to see me, asking that I repeat what I have just said. That led to Taschereau's visit to my niece."

With that, the defence rested. It remained to be seen how much weight the jury would give to all this last-minute evidence.

The Art of Persuasion

It was now time for the lawyers' pleas. The defence had called witnesses and would therefore begin.* Taschereau stood up. As a Quebec City lawyer, he felt his first remarks should be directed toward gaining the respect of the Montreal jury. There had always been a rivalry between the two cities, as indeed there is today. Montreal was Canada's metropolis and one of North America's leading cities; residents of Quebec City fought off their inferiority complex by considering themselves somewhat above Montrealers as citizens of the first city in Canada and the seat of the provincial government. Taschereau broke the ice by explaining that when he first entered the courtroom, "I didn't know the milieu; I was nervous about the task I had accepted and wasn't familiar with the people I would be meeting. But after spending a month with the officers of the Crown, and with my learned friends for the defence, my anxiety and fear slowly disappeared."

After pointing out that "this is the most extraordinary case which has been submitted to a jury in this province and perhaps in all of Canada," he reminded the jury that under the management of the accused the late Alfred Delorme's fortune had grown from $185,000 to $250,000 in six years. During all that time, he added, "Raoul never asked Adélard to account for his management. Indeed, it was under Adélard's enlightened direction that Raoul was at the University of Ottawa preparing himself to take over that management."

The lawyer next all but accused Farah-Lajoie of fabricating evidence: "If a detective is dishonest, he can fabricate his evidence and

---

* The summing up rules of the Criminal Code stipulate that "where no witnesses are examined for an accused, he or his counsel is entitled to address the jury last, but otherwise counsel for the prosecution is entitled to address the jury last."

bring an innocent person before the courts ... when all we have is circumstantial evidence, as in this case, when all we have is a few drops of blood, a pistol, some pieces of rope and a few contradictions, what should we think? Especially when the detective in charge of the case declares that he wants the accused convicted at all costs. What can we think, gentlemen, of the evidence put forward by a detective who, despite being forewarned, acts in a way which the judge has so justly qualified as deplorable? What should we think of all this, gentlemen? Well, if the law allows the jury to judge the accused, it also allows it to judge the accuser."

Taschereau claimed the Crown was wrong in focusing on Delorme's interest in the estate as a motive. "What about the motive of theft? Oh! no, says the Crown, it couldn't be that. It has to be the deficit, nothing else. The accountant Marien found a deficit of $12,000 in the estate but a surplus in Raoul's assets. Is that enough to say that the accused mismanaged his father's estate? He gives his brother a surplus and he suffers a deficit. What does accountant Marien know about the arrangements that may have existed between Adélard and Raoul?" Taschereau reminded the jury that Raoul was wealthier than his brother but paid none of the travelling expenses or the house repairs, all of which were charged to the estate. In those circumstances, it stood to reason that Delorme's affairs might show a deficit. "If the accused had charged Raoul his fair share, Raoul's assets would have been much less. Adélard was intentionally enhancing Raoul's assets at the expense of his own."

Taschereau then spoke of Alfred Delorme's will, in which he had encouraged the family to continue to live together in peace, harmony, and affection. "Is it reasonable to ask the accused to render an accounting as exact as the Royal Trust or the Bank of Montreal? Gentlemen of the jury, the accused sacrificed himself for his brother and his sisters as a good father would. What interest did the accused have in committing that crime? Everyone was living together happily, a new car had just been purchased and tuned up for the trip to Florida that coming summer. Life looked wonderful."

He argued that the Crown hadn't been able to tie the life insurance policy to the murder and asked why everyone was so excited about Raoul making his brother the main beneficiary and sole executor of his will. "Does that mean that for the accused to be innocent, Raoul should have made his will in favour of strangers? Or does it mean that he should have bequeathed his fortune to Lilly and Florence, who couldn't administer it? Or should he have left it to Rosa, who didn't need it? Why not leave it to the accused? Wasn't it he who had raised Raoul, who had given him all the signs of affection that a father would have given his son? Isn't it perfectly natural that Raoul would have thought of him? Wouldn't it have been the height of ingratitude to do the contrary? And yet such an unnatural act would be necessary if the accused is to be found not guilty of his brother's murder. At least, this is what is required by the theories of the Farah-Lajoies, the Pigeons, and the Desgroseillers – of Farah-Lajoie, who has distinguished himself by his relentlessness and who you all know is a cunning man; of Pigeon, who is nothing but a pawn in Farah-Lajoie's hand; and of Desgroseillers, who does nothing but listen to Pigeon." Suggesting that Delorme would not even be on trial if he had not attracted so much attention and cooperated with the police, the lawyer added "and because he spoke this way, because he said these things, because he gave those explanations, they say he's guilty and after two years of martyrdom they drag him before you because he said: 'I have a will made in my favour. I hope Raoul did not forget me, I was so good to him!'"

He spoke of the accused's statement to Farah-Lajoie on 9 January that Raoul had been shot six times and the Crown's attempt to translate this into proof that he must have shot his brother, since that fact was not disclosed before the preliminary hearing in March. Taschereau claimed the information had already been released by a newspaper, adding, "But Delorme didn't have the right to know that, I suppose, and because they don't want to acknowledge that right, they say, 'He must have been the killer.' It is easy to see that such kind of logic self destructs."

Taschereau then reviewed the activities of the Delorme family on the feast of the Epiphany, claiming there was uncontradicted evidence that Raoul was not at home during the afternoon and that there were too many people there in the early evening for any murder to have happened at that time. He acknowledged that from about nine o'clock on, after Florence went out, Delorme could have been alone, but he was convinced that nothing unusual could have happened because the neighbours would have heard something. "I say that it was physically impossible for him to have committed the crime. We can reach that conclusion without hesitation. I say that Raoul Delorme could not have been killed at home."

Convinced that the watch had not been sent to Lorrain by his client, Taschereau seized the opportunity to once again point a finger at Farah-Lajoie. "Why," he asked, "would the accused have left a piece of the chain on his brother's vest but taken the watch and the other end of the chain to send to Chief Lorrain? Such a theory is absurd, because it means Father Delorme would have put the police on his trail. Why would he want to do that? In a city like this, where detectives seem to have an unbridled devotion to their work, why didn't Chief Lorrain take fingerprints from the box?"

As to the bullets, Taschereau derided gunsmith Haynes' testimony, saying he was totally confused in identifying them. He even suggested there may have been some kind of a switch in the bullets. On the other hand, he said, defence testimony "clearly showed the bullets to have been fired by two different pistols."

Taschereau finished on a dramatic note. "Did you see the mannequin that was in the courtroom when the accused's young sisters came to testify? Did you see the torn shirt, the coat and tie still covered with the blood of their brother? When I saw the girls come into the courtroom it seemed as if the shadow of Raoul Delorme was passing through this hall to implore: 'No, no, he's not the one, because if so my sisters would not be here, or if they were, it would be to avenge me.' That dead person is asking you through my mouth to release this man who has been persecuted for the last few weeks. Condemning him would not be an example to society, because he is not guilty." Sounding more like a preacher than a lawyer, Taschereau spoke to the accused, "You have met your persecutors, Adélard Delorme, but if justice is brutal, it is as just as it is stern. You have finished climbing this Calvary on which you have left shreds of flesh and honour, but once at the top, above us, above the jury and above everyone, please say to your enemies that if you have suffered you do not harbour them any ill will." And, turning to the jury, "Through Raoul's voice, through the voice of his little sisters, through the voice of all these witnesses who came to prove their innocence, I now come to ask you to render a verdict of not guilty."

Taschereau had been at his persuasive best, at times cool and logical, at other times pulling at the juror's heart strings. At one point he had even brought tears to some of the jurors' eyes and had had Delorme sobbing like a child. It was clear that Calder's work was cut out for him – and Cahan had yet to be heard! It was late in the day and Lemieux adjourned the court.

The next morning Cahan took the floor. His colleague had spoken in French. Cahan would speak in English. Adopting the same strategy as Taschereau, he repeated most of what he had said, as well as filling in some gaps here and there.

He insisted the murder site couldn't possibly have been the Delorme house. "After I visited the basement, it took me about twenty minutes to wipe dust off my clothes. How would it be possible for the accused to carry Raoul's body along the corridors to the garage without getting any dust on his clothes?" Challenging the credibility of the blood tests, he added, "As to the three or four small blood stains, how could it be concluded that they were human blood? Our methods of blood testing are not sufficiently developed for a case like this one. Furthermore, this is not the type of thing where we should rely on the memory or imagination of witnesses. Mrs Vincent came and told us that her little girl had a nosebleed in the accused's car. All we have to do is rely on her testimony – it isn't necessary to go out and get experts to testify to the nature of the stains." He explained the accused's early knowledge about the six bullets by pointing out that the information had already been published by *The Montreal Daily Star*.

He, too, ended his remarks dramatically, "Gentlemen of the jury, I feel very moved to be involved in a case as important as this one. I almost feel compelled to get on my knees and ask God to bring the truth out of the mouths of witnesses. I think the representatives of the Crown feel the same sense of responsibility. I want to tell you this before I sit down. You're going to go back home tomorrow or the day after. You're going to rest and, as in the past, lay your heads on your pillows after having said your evening prayers. Now I want you to reflect very seriously on your verdict. You cannot condemn the accused unless you are absolutely sure he is guilty. Your conscience dictates an acquittal. I don't know very much about the clergy here, but during the meetings I had with the accused, I could see that he was a proud and distinguished man and that he suffered greatly from the suspicion and doubt that some people allowed to hang over him. There is one thing I hope for. It is that in a few months, or in a few years perhaps, we will find out the truth about this mystery. There is a God up there who will reveal it to us humans."

Visibly exhausted, his face covered with sweat, Cahan crumbled into his seat. He had played his part well and the jury and the Montreal public were aware that a prominent Anglo-Saxon Protestant was energetically defending a French-Canadian Roman Catholic priest.

After the noon break it was Calder's turn. Methodically and logically he connected all the parts of the puzzle. Starting his plea in English, he told the jury this was his tenth murder trial. "In the nine others, as defence counsel I had the good fortune of saving all of my clients from the scaffold. In this case the crime was committed so methodically in such cold blood, with such well calculated premeditation, and later so well hidden that the Crown could not produce direct evidence." The Crown, Calder said, had intentionally arranged the sequence of its witnesses so that very few, if any, could gauge the significance of his or her testimony in the overall scheme of things because "a witness who testifies about a fact without knowing its consequences is a good witness. In that context, circumstantial evidence is often stronger than direct eyewitness evidence."

He had organized his plea as a series of questions. "If you answer yes with me, you will find the accused guilty. If you answer no, you must acquit him."

"What caused Raoul Delorme's death?

"Bullets caused Raoul's death. Not all of them would have killed him, but each left its mark. Each tells its story. One entered his chin and broke it, but it didn't take much of the victim's strength away. Another bullet was lost, travelling through his Adam's apple. That bullet disabled its victim, somewhat like a knockout punch, but it wasn't mortal. Another bullet penetrated his mouth, blowing away some bone splinters from the floor of his palate. That bullet wasn't found. The forensic surgeons believe that Raoul spit it out in his last agonizing gasps. But then are the two killer bullets. They were shot from in front of the victim and lodged in his spine. One of them grazed the pneumogastric nerve and stopped his heart.

"Where were the bullets found?

"Three bullets were found, two during the first autopsy, a third during the second. The first two were examined by Dr Derome and gunsmith Haynes. The bullet fired out of Haynes' Bayard served as a comparison for the bullets found in the body. It's been said that Detective Farah-Lajoie manipulated that bullet. I won't defend Detective Farah-Lajoie. I will simply say that the best police officers are often attacked. And the better they are, the more they are attacked. It was said that bullet fired from the gunsmith's Bayard may have been faked. I ask you, how could it possibly have been faked to become identical with the bullet which was then in Raoul's body in the cemetery? The bullets were shown to you in photographic enlargements made under a microscope. We showed you the ridges, the unusual scratches, their similarities, all of which were measured with a micrometer. You are still free to examine them with that equipment to see who is right. Two Bayard pistols were fired, one belonging to Mr Haynes and the other to the accused. The ridges are the same. So you must either accuse Mr Haynes of the murder or you must accuse the man at the bar. Mr Jones, who I publicly acknowledged to be a competent and honest man, came to testify. But did he make the experiments himself, did he take the measurements himself? No. You know that he was assisted by a Mr Hamilton who the defence was afraid to call as a witness and who Mr Jones, as an honest expert, clearly did not recommend. And what about the oil on the revolver? When Haynes sold it to the accused, it was tested and proved to be in perfect working order. He then cleaned it before handing it over to the accused. Haynes next saw it when the police brought it back to his shop in mid-January. It was then heavily oiled – far more so than when he had sold it to the accused. We must therefore believe that the revolver was used and immediately afterwards heavily oiled to cast away any suspicions. And what about the unexplained ten missing bullets. Haynes sold the accused two boxes of twenty-five bullets each on 27 December. At that same time, eight of those bullets were used in his target range to demonstrate the action of the Bayard. Yet in mid-January, when the police brought the Bayard and boxes to Haynes shop for identification, there were only twenty-eight bullets in the boxes. That means fourteen bullets were used. We know that four were used by the police for subsequent tests but no one has explained what happened to the other ten.

"Where was the murder committed?

"I say Raoul was murdered at 190 St Hubert Street. First, because of his overshoes which stayed at home. And his sisters admitted he had no others. The cobbler who had varnished the soles of his shoes two days earlier testified that it would have been impossible to walk on snow or ice for more than five minutes without wearing off that varnish. Perhaps Raoul did leave the house marching like a policeman, as has been testified, but he came back and when he went out again, it was feet first. He wasn't wearing his overcoat when he was shot, otherwise it would have been pierced by bullets, as was his jacket. The quilt around his head was identical from every point of view – texture, material, overall make-up – with two quilts found at Delorme's home. So I conclude that the crime was committed at home. Mr Taschereau said he believed the testimony of the accused's sisters. He admitted that if the crime had been committed at home it could only have been committed by one person. It certainly couldn't have been Rosa, Lilly, or Florence. But would the sisters incriminate their brother? I myself would commit perjury rather than condemn my brother. I believe, however, that they generally told the truth except for two small questions.

"In what part of the house was it committed?

"The defence said that it couldn't have been in the basement, garage, or kitchen because the shots would have been heard by the neighbours. But in the sitting room, the situation is different. It has a brick wall thick enough to prevent noise from going through. That room is where Raoul spent most of his time reading and smoking his pipe. That's where the crime was committed. The defence disagrees because there were no bullet holes in the walls. Two experts have testified that the bullets would have lost their force after having gone through Raoul's body and would possibly have fallen on the floor, where the accused could have picked them up. Let's not forget that it was not until late January that the detectives made their first search of the Delorme home. So the accused had ample time to clean up and dispose of any evidence.

"Delorme testified that he was in the basement around 10:30, but witnesses have sworn that slightly after eleven o'clock they heard a car leaving the Delorme garage. And remember Woods, who saw the car on Décarie Boulevard."

Calder suggested that the murder had been committed while Adélard was alone at home either between 3:45 and 4:45 on the afternoon or 9:00 and 10:00 in the evening, if Lilly was telling the truth when she said she was home all afternoon. "It is equally believable that it happened in the afternoon and that Lilly was not there, despite her testimony to the contrary. What she said matters little because, under oath, she categorically denied her own testimony given a few moments earlier. You are entitled to disregard her testimony because it has been proven that she cannot be believed, even under oath. Furthermore, the time of the murder matters little if you are convinced that it was committed in the house.

"What was the motive?

"Defence counsel has said there is no motive in this case. I say there is one. Raoul Delorme fell under a barrage of bullets so the accused could become richer by $185,000. The defence has said that no one would ever commit such a foul deed on his own brother. And who was the first murderer? Cain killed Abel, his younger brother, for much less."

In closing, Calder knew he had to wrestle with the touchy question of the jury's religious beliefs. "There was once in France a case as sad as this one. I will not recount its details, but one day, thinking to please the Church, a guilty priest was withdrawn from the hands of justice. From that day, a wave of anti-clericalism began to rise in France and from that incident began the terrible trials the Catholic Church has had to go through in that country. It was not the act of the Church, it was the act of the state wishing to please the Church. The end result was that the Church was the biggest victim. Gentlemen, I was taught by the Jesuits. I recently attended an alumni meeting where I met with many of my former professors. They all encouraged me to carry out my duty, whatever the consequences. I would not have expected anything else from those who taught me the value of integrity and honesty, which may not have made me a rich man but has kept me proud. Among the twelve apostles there was Judas. Yet Christianity lives. The Church has had bad priests, yet the Church still stands."

After a brief adjournment Calder repeated his plea in French. By the time he sat down, he had spoken for five hours to a rather inattentive jury. The judge adjourned.

At the crack of dawn on Saturday, 21 July, a queue started forming in front of the courthouse. The crowd was abuzz with speculation. It was close to eleven o'clock by the time the 900 spectators got settled down in the courtroom built to accommodate 300. Judge Lemieux began his address by paying homage to the late judge Dominique Monet who "died of exhaustion, no doubt partly due to the rigours and demands of last year's insanity trial which, against his doctor's orders, he energetically presided over with the high intellectual capacity and integrity which was so characteristic of him." The judge then looked straight at the jury and pointing at the accused, asked, "Is Adélard Delorme guilty of his half-brother's murder? Is it he who, on the night of 6 January 1922, shot and killed that unfortunate young man?"

The judge explained that intent to kill was essential to the legal definition of murder. "A murderer always has a motive. He kills for vengeance, hate, greed, or out of self-interest." He warned the jury not to be overly concerned with some of the contradictory evidence about times, dates, and places. Contradictions exist in all trials. "What has to be done in any trial is to consider the facts taken as a whole and try to arrive at a conscientious and reasonable conclusion."

He said the carefully wrapped body showed that the murder was not the work of highway robbers. "If not, " he asked, "then who would have taken such precautions? Surely someone who wanted to avoid the spreading of bloodstains. So who is that person?"

He then reviewed the evidence about Raoul's fortune and stressed the fact that Raoul had no known enemies. "Raoul was the youngest in the family. The accused was the eldest. Blood line and the law made of the eldest, Adélard, his younger brother's natural protector. Was he?"

To the great satisfaction of Farah-Lajoie, Judge Lemieux seemed to be pointing a finger at Delorme. "The accused bought a pistol on 27 December 1921. It was a 25-calibre Bayard automatic pistol with an almost silent detonator, rapid firing ability, and easy to handle. Has the defence proven that the accused needed a firearm? Had his peace and tranquillity been threatened? Did he fear an attack? Did he intend to travel to faraway places? Did he make dangerous nocturnal trips? We have no explanations. As a general rule a well-respected priest does not need a firearm to protect himself, even in a city as big as Montreal."

The judge spoke about the car. "A car was used to transport the body. The accused has one and he is or must have been a good driver, capable of driving a car at night and, within a relatively short time, taking the body to where it was found. Did he do that? It is not enough to say that a man is capable of doing something, it has to be proven." Reviewing the testimony of Delorme's neighbours he added, "All of that evidence demonstrates that the accused stayed up late that night, that he did something in his garage, and that he started his car engine. Why would he do such things at that time of the night? It is up to you to answer."

Then he talked about the bullets and explained that Delorme had to be found guilty if the bullets in Raoul's body had been fired from his Bayard. He spoke highly of the Crown's experts. "They are disinterested, competent, and impartial witnesses who enlightened the judge and jury. They are not biased." He gave little credibility to Jones and reminded them that "his associate Hamilton is a man of dubious reputation."

His remarks about the blood found on the car cushions had a touch of sarcasm. "You will have to admit, gentlemen of the jury, that the accused's automobile was an unlucky one – three times within the space of two months the cushions were stained by the blood of three different people. It's a car I would hesitate to get into, for fear of getting a nosebleed. The question now is to determine if the cushions and seat of the car were stained a fourth time on the night of 6 January by the blood of the victim, Raoul Delorme. It's up to you to give the answer."

Judge Lemieux thought the Crown had presented strong evidence about the quilts in the Delorme house being identical to those on Raoul's head. He questioned Rosa's testimony that the family's only quilts were those found in the house and that she hadn't seen any other similar ones in over twenty years. "She never saw any others? That is evidence which you would have to accept without hesitation if it had been given by a more independent and more impartial witness than young Rosa Delorme. But, you see, this young girl comes here to testify in favour of whom? In favour of her brother, who is a priest; in favour of her brother who is now accused of murder; in favour of her brother who, if condemned, will suffer capital punishment. If your child was accused of murder, would you be inclined to swear in his favour?"

The judge seemed convinced Delorme had addressed the package delivered to Lorrain. "Isn't it a singular, a very singular coincidence, that this handwriting so greatly resembles the accused's?" He also found it strange that Raoul wasn't wearing overshoes. "One does not go out in that cold without overshoes. So why wasn't Raoul wearing any? Why were they found a few days later under the clothes rack in the Delorme house? Could it be that Raoul came back home and that his killer, while dressing him, forgot to put them back on? That's a serious question gentlemen of the jury, which only you have the power to answer."

He didn't believe the testimony about Raoul being in Côte Saint-Michel. The evidence was far too weak. As to the testimony of the two nightclub employees, "whose lifestyle is somewhat suspect," he came as close as he could to saying they had committed perjury.

Judge Lemieux cautioned the jury about being influenced by the accused's apparent cooperation with the police. "It was in his interest to cooperate, the contrary would have invited suspicion. Sooner or later the police would have heard about the Bayard purchased at Haynes' gun shop. Such a lie would have been far more compromising for the accused."

Seeming to lean towards a conviction he continued by almost categorically endorsing the Crown's argument that the accused had killed his brother to get at his fortune. "The history of crime shows very many criminals to have killed for much less," he said. "Killers have been known to kill their father for $50, some have killed their neighbours for $200. Why should we have difficulty believing that an evil and greedy man would kill for $185,000?"

He, too, ended his address by commenting on the religious question. "Gentlemen, I can understand in my heart, in the heart of an experienced old man, that you would have fears and apprehensions before pronouncing a verdict of guilt. I understand those fears. They demonstrate in you the respect so legitimately due to our clergy, to whom our people owes its national survival more than to any other factor. My friends, that hesitation attests that for you a priest who is good, I repeat, when he is good, chaste and virtuous, when he is inspired by the teachings of Christ, is indeed the moral support of our society, the comforter of afflicted souls, the secure guide of our youth, and the wise counsellor of our Christian families. I understand your hesitation. I also understand the deep humiliation the Roman Catholic Church must be going through in seeing one of its own ministers accused of an infamous crime. What a downfall, my friends, what a downfall! To leave the altar where the accused offered the Holy Sacrifice – Oh no – to leave the confessional where he absolves the sins of others to flounder at the bar of justice like habitual criminals, bandits, and evil-doers. What a decline, what a downfall.

But, the Roman Catholic Church is too majestic a society, she has too great a past ... for the ignominious fault of one of her ministers to cause her to lose her hold on the hearts and souls of her faithful. The Church would lose some of its prestige, some of its respect, if it were said that in a great district like Montreal, which includes one million souls, she could not allow twelve jurors to condemn a priest if the evidence established him to be a murderer. Gentlemen of the jury, being convinced of the accused's guilt and acquitting him because of his priestly character would be to make yourselves the accomplice of a dishonest priest and of a fratricide. The Roman Catholic Church, just like the law, would condemn such complacency as an abominable crime, an infamy. On the other hand, this accused man who is a priest has the right to all the privileges and advantages that the law gives its British subjects. He has the right to ask the jury for an acquittal if the evidence is not conclusive beyond any reasonable doubt. But the doubt must be a serious one, a thoughtful and conscientious one. It must be neither artificial, nor imaginary, nor created solely to discard a responsibility. Jurists have defined reasonable doubt as a wavering uncertainty or indecisiveness in one's mind for lack of sufficient evidence. If after your deliberations you find yourselves in that state of mind, then you must acquit the accused. May the Angel of Divine Justice inspire you to render a verdict in accordance with the evidence and may God help you, gentlemen."

It was 1:30. Judge Lemieux had spoken for over two hours. He would now have to repeat his remarks in English. To catch his breath, he adjourned until 3:15. Before leaving the prisoner's dock, Delorme was overheard commenting to Cahan, "It's tough, but all will go well anyway."

When the court reconvened, the accused seemed rather bored by the judge's remarks in English and yawned repeatedly until finally dozing off. The judge ended his remarks shortly before 5:30 and adjourned until nine o'clock, asking the jury to try to reach a verdict by then. As Delorme was led away, he waved confidently at Rosa who, except for a few female reporters from the United States, was the only woman left in the audience.

By dinnertime, a crowd of about 5,000 had gathered in and around the Court-house waiting for the decision. About 900 had been lucky enough to squeeze into the courtroom. Iron restraining bars had had to be installed across the corridor to hold back the surging mob. At nine o'clock Delorme was led into the prisoner's dock with Prison Governor Séguin at his side. A few moments later Judge Lemieux entered. A tense and silent courtroom waited. Finally, after fifteen minutes the jury made its entrance. Once seated the clerk took the roll call and asked in both French and English, "Have you agreed on a verdict? What say you? Do you find the prisoner at the bar who is accused of the murder of Raoul Delorme guilty or not guilty?" Wilfrid David rose from his seat and answered, "I must declare that the jury is not in agreement and after having discussed the matter between us, I believe that we will be unable to reach agreement."

The courtroom sat in stunned silence. Farah-Lajoie couldn't believe his ears. Delorme smiled. After a few moments, Judge Lemieux broke the tension. "Gentlemen, I am not surprised that you disagree, you had only three hours to deliberate. The greatest judge in the world would not have reached a decision in this case before having deliberated for at least twenty days. If I were to accept your disagreement at this point, after a hearing of thirty-two days and evidence from 173 witnesses, the whole country would be dissatisfied and the jury system might be in peril. The court requests that you deliberate further. The law permits you to render a verdict on Sunday. If you reach agreement before Monday, advise the sheriff and he will see to it that we hold an emergency session." The jury shuffled back to the jury room.

Sunday went by without any news. Finally, at about 10:15 on Monday morning, 23 July, the judge took his seat, followed a few moments later by Delorme and the jury. Delorme was smiling and relaxed, looking more like a spectator than a person who was facing the gallows. The clerk asked the jury if it reached a decision. David replied, "I must declare that we have been unable to reach agreement."

Judge Lemieux was beyond himself and had no intention of letting the jury off easily. "Gentlemen, of the jury," he said in an exasperated tone, "the Court still hopes that you will agree and is not convinced that you cannot. To avoid public accusations that you have not thoroughly studied the case, I will adjourn until three o'clock this afternoon. You must understand that the result of your disagreement would be to send the accused back to prison to submit to a new trial, which would be very costly not only for him but also for the public. I know you will reach a conclusion."

The delay didn't help. When the court reconvened, the jury foreman stated, almost embarrassed, "Your Lordship, in the name of the jury

I must declare that we are still unable to reach an agreement and that we believe it useless to deliberate any longer because it will not change the result." A resigned Lemieux replied, "In the circumstances the Court discharges you." Taschereau immediately asked that the accused be released on his personal cognizance. His request was denied.

Cahan asked to speak. Visibly disturbed, he criticized the Crown for appealing to religious bias. Calder jumped to his feet and bitterly rebutted. Before matters got worse, Judge Lemieux ended the debate by diplomatically interjecting, "Before leaving this courtroom I want to compliment the lawyers, the members of the press, and the jury."

Accompanied by his ever-present bodyguard, Governor Séguin, Delorme was immediately driven to Bordeaux Prison where he would stay until his new trial. It was later learned that he was sure of an acquittal and had made arrangements to spruce up 190 St Hubert Street for his return, as well as to travel to Quebec City with Dr Brochu for a few days rest. But he had taken the jury's indecision rather calmly. Under the large front page headline "Jury Dismissed," The *Montreal Daily Star* reported "Delorme might have been listening to a debate on the cosmological implications of redemption, for all the effect the jury's disagreement had upon him, so far as one could see."

Outside the courtroom, the jury talked openly to the press. It was learned that the count had been eight to four for a guilty verdict after Taschereau's address, increasing to nine after Calder's remarks, and to ten after the judge's. It didn't change from that until they were finally discharged. The 24 July edition of the *New York Times* reported that Judge Lemieux had discharged the jury after "rebuking them for the expense they had cost the people." The story went on to state that P.D. Décarie, one of the jurors, had told reporters that he and W.D. David stood for acquittal against the other ten. He was quoted as saying, "After hearing the entire speech of the learned judge, I was sure that the accused was not guilty. I stuck to that theory through the entire time that the jury was debating. Two of us were for acquitting him while the rest were confident that the accused was guilty." The *Montreal Gazette* quoted some jurors as having said "the tide for and against conviction had ebbed and flowed."*

* The jurymen in favour of a guilty verdict were William Hughes, Emery Dansereau, H.F.B. Powell, Georges Corriveau, Dr. J.S. Tiffany, Alfred Plourde, Alexis Prévost, William Niddell, Jules Goyer, and Daniel Guimond. The two who favoured acquittal were Wilfrid David (the foreman) and P. Décarie. Today, it is a criminal offence in Canada for members of a jury to discuss their deliberations or otherwise disclose any information relating to their proceedings, unless disclosed in open court.

Once again there was a public outcry. *La Presse* commented:

Three times Delorme's peers declared that they could not agree on their verdict, forcing Sir François Lemieux to adjourn the case to the next term of the Assizes, in September. This is the outcome (or rather the lack of outcome) of a trial which has impassioned Montreal and the province more than any other in our judicial annals, mainly because of the character of the accused and the mystery which surrounds the murder, which, as Mr Cahan said, has caused tremors in one of our most deeply rooted social convictions. It was memorable trial with memorable incidents and memorable speeches, during the course of which the lawyers displayed their ability to use every conceivable skill in legal strategy, often adjusting to deal with unforeseen events, always convincing in their logic and moving in their eloquence.

Comments were made about Delorme's extraordinary energy, his confidence, and his many interruptions during the trial. One of the writers from *La Presse* even wrote:

He resisted with steel nerves, seemingly more by stubbornness than will-power. He always looked at the humorous side of things, even when the jury was about to pronounce a sentence which might send him to the scaffold. He had extraordinary perspicacity, which permitted him to follow everything that was going on between the lawyers, judge, and jury without for a moment losing sight of what was happening in the audience.

Although the case gradually moved off the front pages, there continued to be daily developments. The police reported the reappearance of Leclerc and of a witness who claimed Raoul was killed during a card game at Côte Saint-Michel.

Alleyn Taschereau asked the Premier of Quebec to hold the next trial in Quebec city. Rumour had it that it would be held in either St Jean or St Hyacinthe because of the impossibility of finding an objective jury in Montreal. Judge Lemieux refused to have any more to do with the case. "I did my duty in helping the Department of Justice unravel this affair. I imposed heavy sacrifices on myself. It's now another judge's turn."

Throughout the summer Gustave Monette persisted in trying to have Delorme declared unfit for trial. His petitions to the attorney general and premier of Quebec were of no avail. Finally, it was announced that the trial would be held in November and that, to accelerate things, it would be conducted only in French.

On 5 November, Delorme once again stood in the prisoner's dock. It was obvious that he had not suffered from his special lifestyle at Bordeaux Prison. As reported in *La Presse*:

Although his hair had turned somewhat grey, he had a ruddy complexion and was the picture of health. He smiled at some of the friends he recognized in the courtroom and blew a kiss to his sister Rosa. The audience included Farah-Lajoie and Wilfrid David, the jury foreman who had voted for an acquittal at the 1922 trial.

Calder told the court that he was ready to proceed. Due to a lack of funds, defence counsel Alleyn Taschereau asked for a postponement until January. It was granted. Another factor was Cahan's withdrawal. "Since the next trial will be totally in French," he told the press, "I don't consider I know the language well enough to continue, and although no one has a greater respect than I do for the Roman Catholic faith, I am convinced that a French Canadian Catholic lawyer will be able to defend the accused far better than I who am English and Protestant." No longer involved, Cahan felt he could get something off his chest. On 28 January 1924 he wrote to the attorney general of Quebec severely criticizing the judge and crown prosecutor: "What possible relevancy to the issues involved in this trial could so grotesque an account of the rise of anti-clericalism in France possibly have? By what right, moral, political, or legal, does a representative of the Crown suggest to faithful Catholic jurymen that it is their duty to condemn Abbé Delorme in order to resist a possible or probable wave of anti-clericalism in the province of Quebec?" Cahan ended his letter with these words: "The proceedings rendered it quite impossible to procure from the jury an unbiased verdict upon the facts adduced in evidence."

Déjà Vu

The courtroom was only half filled when the third trial got under way on 25 February 1924. This time the heading of the next morning's story in The *Gazette* headline read "Absence of pomp marked opening of Delorme trial," as it reported,

With considerably less of the picturesque formality which featured the beginning of the last trial of Reverend Father Adélard Delorme, the second trial was opened yesterday morning in the Court of King's Bench, Mr Justice Martineau presiding. If the first day was not so taken up with the decorous formalities as on the last occasion, it was more businesslike.

A new cast of jurists appeared on the scene. The defence counsel was now the fiery Alban Germain, one of the leading criminal lawyers in the country. A dramatic-looking man of forty-eight with piercing eyes and a huge curly mustache, Germain was a spellbinder. There was no better man when it came to swaying a jury.* He was assisted by Lucien Gendron, also known for his great eloquence. On the bench sat the Honourable Paul Gédéon Martineau. With a Doctorate in Law from McGill, he was greatly respected within the legal profession. Other than Robert Calder, the only familiar face at counsel's table was that of Gustave Monette. When asked how he pleaded, Delorme bit into each word as he answered "Not guilty." As expected, Monette made his plea of insanity. Just as expectedly, it was rejected.

---

* A colourful chain-smoking and hard-drinking character, Germain was then at the height of his ability. His lifestyle eventually effected his work and he ended his days living on handouts. He died tragically at sixty-seven, the victim of a fire in his home accidently set by his burning cigarette.

By noon the jury, this time totally French-speaking, had been chosen.* After the adjournment, the Delorme sisters testified for close to two hours and repeated the story they had told eight months earlier. But they had polished up the rough spots. There was far less hesitation and more precision in what they said. On balance, the accused appeared happy with his sisters – they had been well prepared. The trial proceeded quickly for the first two days. The same cast of witnesses was heard but this time almost without cross-examination. It was obvious that everyone was anxious to get the trial over.

That pattern was broken on the third day when the Crown produced a surprise witness. Édouard Dépocas told the court that he had seen the accused driving his car at 2:00 A.M. on 7 January 1922 near the entrance of Côte des Neiges Cemetery. Dépocas, who lived on Gatineau street in front of the cemetery, said he saw the car slow down and stop for a moment opposite his front door. "I could see by his roman collar that the driver was a priest. I thought he was returning home from late night visits. The car was heading towards Snowdon. I could almost positively recognize his profile. He was stopped under a street light. I noticed a second occupant sitting in the back seat, slouched to the side."

The accused turned ashen as he listened to Dépocas. He appeared stunned and, for the first time since the discovery of Raoul's body, he seemed frightened. He listened apprehensively as Dépocas explained that he was watching very closely because the car had inadvertently followed the tramway rails which, at that particular spot, veered away from the street into a wooded area. "That kind of accident happens quite often in the winter when snow covers the rails and gives them the appearance of a snow covered street. After a few feet, drivers normally realize what has happened and back up." Dépocas clearly identified the car as Delorme's, which he just examined at the municipal garage. The fact that he was a car dealer gave that identification added credibility.

A few days into the trial the jury complained that someone was spying on them through the skylight of the jury room on the top floor of the court house.† Germain, assuming that the spy was a security employee of the sheriff's office, and therefore of the Crown,

---

* The jury was composed of Messrs R. Thibault, Georges Larose, J.O. Caron, E. Grandbois, F. Chartier, L.P. Dufresne, L.S. Lamoureux, E. Longpré, Eugène Bastien, J. Parent, E. Deragon, L. Lecavalier.
† In those years, the top floor of the Court-house was set aside as living quarters for the jury.

commented: "I think it would be only fair that the defence be made aware of attempts to protect the jury. Sometimes such protection can be dangerous." Calder did not appreciate the insinuation and challenged Germain, who eventually backed off, saying, "I am convinced that if the sheriff knew of any incidents [where information had been passed to the prosecution] he would be the first to regret it. However he should be careful that his efforts to protect the jury are not mistaken for spying."

As in the 1923 trial, the Crown wanted Delorme's deposition at the coroner's inquest read into the record. Germain objected, invoking the noncompellable witness rule. He went even further: he objected to any of Delorme's statements to police officials being part of the evidence on the basis that they were made to persons in authority and were not free and voluntary. To succeed in this objection he needed to establish that, among other things, the police had suspected the accused from their first contact with him. He demanded to examine the detectives on *voir dire* and with the exclusion of the jury, which was granted. He then called Detective Pigeon to the stand.

"You told us that on 7 January, when you talked in Chief Lepage's office, you did not in any way suspect the reverend?

"Absolutely not, I didn't suspect him."

"And you were not in the process of arresting him?"

"No."

"And you did not even suspect that he could be arrested?"

"No sir."

"Could you tell us the exact date on which you began suspecting him?"

"The fourteenth."

"Of which month?"

"Of January 1922."

"As a result of what incident?"

"Because we learned that he had purchased a handgun at Mr Haynes' on 27 December."

"And from that moment did you suspect him?"

"Yes, sir."

"And you kept a surveillance on him with the view of arrest?"

"Yes."

"Up until that moment, did you suspect him?"

"No."

The witness further stated that on 7, 8, and 9 January, when he and his colleagues examined the Delorme house, they were not looking for evidence against the priest but simply something which might

help them in their investigation. He said the same applied to their
questions to Rosa, Florence, Lilly. He added that there was no indication that any of the other detectives or police involved in the case
suspected the priest before the fourteenth. Their many visits were
not because they suspected Delorme, he said, but because he invited
them over and volunteered information to them. When they looked
around the house, Delorme insisted on accompanying them to give
them additional information.

Georges Farah-Lajoie came to the stand and said he had been
assigned to the case on 10:00 A.M. 9 January 1922. He, too, confirmed
that he began to suspect Delorme on 14 January when they learned
about the handgun. He said that he considered the information
supplied to them by Delorme as freely given. It was definitely not
preceded by any promises or threats. He admitted that he might have
had some small doubts before the fourteenth but that they certainly
weren't serious enough to be considered as suspicion, adding, "In all
our cases we're given to changing our minds from one moment to
the next." Detective Desgroseillers testified to the same effect. He
was followed to the stand by Chief Lepage, who told the court he
had first met the accused on 7 January after he had identified Raoul's
body at the morgue. "After I presented my condolences he asked me
if I was the chief of detectives and I said I was. So he said "Well, Mr
Chief, and Messrs Detectives, I saw my brother Raoul for the last
time yesterday at lunch. I then did my clerical tasks and around supper
time Raoul called me to say he had met an old friend, a college
classmate, and another person that he didn't know. 'Bring them
home,' I said, and Raoul answered, 'I am not going home tonight but
I will be there tomorrow morning to take the train.'"

Lepage explained that the accused began telephoning him after
Raoul's funeral on the eleventh, saying he had additional information
to supply and asking him to send detectives over. This happened quite
a few times, he said, and at no time was any information extracted
from the accused. To the contrary, he seemed anxious to talk and
appeared proud to be able to help the detectives so much. As a matter
of fact, the accused often seemed to think the detectives were helpless
without him.

Lepage said that the police had become suspicious of Delorme on
14 January. From that date on, Delorme had been watched, at first
rather casually but from the twenty-fourth on he had been under
close surveillance. A police officer accompanied him wherever he
went and spent the night at the Delorme home.

With that, Germain ended his *voir dire*. He argued that the police
had become suspicious of the accused some time between the ninth
and the fourteenth of January and that consequently everything his
client said to the police after the ninth was definitely inadmissible.
Calder countered that the accused had volunteered information to
the police at the drop of a hat and had insisted on testifying before
the coroner, which he did with great enthusiasm.

After due deliberation, Judge Martineau ruled that not only were
Delorme's statements to the police admissible but so was his deposition at the coroner's inquest. Nothing Delorme had said had been
said under duress or with expectation of reward. He had one caveat
and it concerned answers the accused may have given to questions
asked by Farah-Lajoie. He said he would not allow an answer to be
admitted if he felt the question had been asked with the intention of
gathering evidence against Delorme without his knowledge, not
simply to gather information. The ruling was a severe setback for
Germain, who had expected the judge to decide in favor of the
accused, as Lemieux had done in the 1923 trial. The jury was ushered
back into the courtroom and Delorme's deposition was read as an
angry Germain looked on.

Farah-Lajoie, Pigeon, Desgroseillers, and Chief Lepage then took
the stand and essentially repeated the testimony they had given at the
1923 trial, although this time the Crown prosecutor made a point of
having them stress the various deceptive statements the accused had
made to them, particularly concerning the gun and Raoul's will.

During their testimony, the court had to adjourn for Ash Wednesday, a Holy Day of Obligation in the Province of Quebec. The break
came at a good time because the jury was showing signs of restless-
ness. The following story appeared in the 5 March edition of The
Gazette, under the heading "Jurors in Delorme Case Demand Some
More Distractions":

Apart from going to Mass what are the jurymen in the Delorme case going
to do today, Ash Wednesday? The question was asked pointedly by juror
number two yesterday afternoon and his colleagues nodded approvingly.
Mr Justice Martineau suggested that the Sheriff will do everything within
reason and the law to make life a little gay for them. As the murder trial of
Father Adélard Delorme is dragging along, now well into the second week,
and not by any signs half finished yet, the jurymen are showing evidence of
being bored, a little impatient and tired of being constantly together under
the august survey of uniform policemen. On Monday the complaint was

bitterly made that they are being "spied upon" and that they do not get enough hot water for their weekly bath; yesterday the absence of any occupation other than listening to evidence, eating, drinking and sleeping was beginning to tell. When Mr Justice Martineau told the jury that the Sheriff would do anything he could "to give you a little entertainment," jurymen number two replied "The hours are going to be long and dreary" to which the judge answered "Of course, you can go to Mass in the morning."

Furnace stoker Ernest Leclerc finally took the stand for the Crown. He said he had left Montreal in early 1922 to seek work in the U.S. and had just been released from a Vermont prison where he was serving time for theft of a horse and buggy. He told the court that on the Feast of the Epiphany he had gone to the Delorme house three times, first at 11:00 A.M., then at 3:00 P.M., and finally at 9:00 P.M. On his afternoon visit, the furnace was out. He worked on it for about forty-five minutes until it started and returned that evening to make sure it was still burning. Contrary to Delorme's testimony, Leclerc said the furnace was heating properly that evening. He filled it with coal and left. He returned at seven o'clock on the morning of the seventh and found everything in order. When asked if he saw Delorme on his visits, he said he hadn't. He had a key which gave him access to the basement at any time.

The Crown had hoped Leclerc could fill in some of the gaps about what the Delorme family did on the sixth, but not only had Leclerc seen no one, he claimed he hadn't been at the Delorme house during the critical period of four to nine P.M. or after 9:45. On the other hand, he contradicted Delorme's deposition at the coroner's inquest. Delorme had testified then that while he was in his study reading his breviary around ten o'clock he found the house cold and went down to the basement to work on the furnace for about three hours. According to Leclerc, not only was the furnace heating properly when he checked things out at nine but he had found everything in order early the next morning. Since Delorme's testimony had now been heard by the jury, the contradiction was significant. If the furnace was working properly, as Leclerc had testified, what was Delorme doing in the basement for three hours? Calder remembered that at the coroner's inquest Rosa's boyfriend, Davis, had been asked about the temperature in the house that evening. He decided to call him back to the stand. After a short recess Davis took the stand and confirmed that at both seven o'clock, when he called on Rosa to take her and Lilly to the theatre, and at eleven, when he took them home, the Delorme home was comfortably warm.

The Crown's next witness was Dr Derome, whose ballistics evidence was now stronger than ever. "Because of the new operation we performed which permitted us to find another bullet in the victim's mouth, I can now state positively that the eight holes in the skull were caused by six bullets." He then explained an additional test he had made with Delorme's weapon. It consisted of pouring a sulphur-based mixture into the barrel and withdrawing the mould after it had hardened. This procedure faithfully reproduced the marks on the inside of the barrel. It was also learned that since the last trial Haynes had fired two additional bullets with both Delorme's Bayard and the so-called twin Bayard introduced by the defence at the last trial. A comparison with the bullets found in Raoul's body confirmed without a doubt that they had been fired from the accused's gun. While the jury was busy examining the bullets through a microscope, the accused was industriously studying a number of books and holding them well up over the rail of the prisoner's dock to make their titles obvious. One of them was entitled *The Second Congress of Medical Legal Study* and the other *The Art of Shooting.** He read with his lips moving, frequently underlining here and there with a red pencil and marking pages for future reference.

Raoul's skull was then passed among the jury. Derome gave his explanations with a maestro's baton, pointing to a bust provided by the Crown for that purpose. Suddenly, with a rather perplexed look on his face, Judge Martineau interrupted him and asked to take a closer look at the bust, which, by this time, had been liberally marked up by Derome. With a rather amused expression which brought a roar of laughter from the audience, he told Calder and Germain that the bust that was being so liberally scribbled on by the star witness was none other than that of Sir Andrew Stuart, the former chief justice of Quebec. A blushing Calder quickly handed the sculpture to a clerk and whispered a few words to him. The abused bust was immediately rushed out of the courtroom and replaced with another, later identified as that of Mozart. For the next few hours the head of Salzburg's genius was the jury's learning aid.

Delorme's deposition having been read into the record meant that his story about the mysterious late night telephone call was also now part of the evidence. This gave the Crown the opportunity to call employees of the telephone company as witnesses. One of them confirmed

* *Le Deuxième Congrès de la Médecine Légale* and *Le Tir.*

that the calls had been made between 1:00 and 3:00 A.M., but during the night of the tenth to the eleventh of January, not the sixth to the seventh as had been stated by the accused. She confirmed that after the third call Delorme had told her he didn't want to be disturbed any more. She remembered that a fourth call had been received a few minutes later and she had passed it on to her supervisor. The supervisor came to the stand and added that the fourth call was from another telephone booth. "I told him it was useless to insist, that Father Delorme didn't want to be disturbed. After a short discussion, he hung up." The manager of the company corroborated the testimonies, specifying that the calls were made from a phone booth at the Northeastern Lunch Company on St Catherine Street East. The last employee to testify was the operator who had been on duty on the night of the sixth. She had no record of any calls that night and had received no complaints from anyone called Delorme. These testimonies, if true, suggested that Delorme, having told the police on the ninth of January about the calls, might have wanted to protect his story by having someone call the next night. He could then argue that the telephone company was confused about the dates.

The balance of the testimony moved very quickly, much to the delight of the jury. As they sensed that the end was near, their mood became lighter. Indeed on 17 March the totally French Canadian jury became Irish for a day with each member proudly displaying a shamrock on his lapel. Their foreman even offered one to the judge, who accepted happily. By the next day, all of the evidence was in. A huge audience was on hand to hear Alban Germain's plea.

Germain began by stressing that he would not play on the jury's emotions because "that could only lead to prejudice, not justice." He then proceeded to accuse the Crown of prejudice. "More zeal has been displayed in this case, from the attorney general to the lowest ranking policeman, than has been seen in any other case in the history of the province of Quebec. They didn't want it said by our English-speaking compatriots that a priest had been acquitted because of his priesthood. They wanted to avoid suspicion about the impartiality of our race. If they do not want to acquit the accused because he is a priest, they should not make that the reason for being more severe than they would be with a layman."

With the accused's deposition at the coroner's inquest now in evidence, Germain had no choice but to try to turn it to his advantage. He said it showed that Delorme was working alone in the basement and garage from nine to eleven in the evening. That had been corroborated not only by Delorme's three sisters but also by Leclerc.

Germain told the jury, "It is possible that the sisters are not gifted with the best of intelligence, but that's all the more reason to believe their testimony. When the accused was in the basement and his sister called out to him 'Come to bed, it's one o'clock.' are we to believe that those words were all part of a diabolical stageplay produced for the benefit of the accused's defence? Such a conspiracy would surpass human imagination and make Lilly an accomplice. I refuse to believe such a monstrosity. I refuse to believe that a man who for years held the Holy Host in his hands would commit an act that Satan himself would refuse to commit."

Germain ridiculed Dépocas' testimony. "How could he identify the accused's profile from his roman collar? A roman collar isn't like a face, it doesn't have a profile." He found it bizarre that the police had searched the Delorme house about twenty times before they found the piece of rope in the basement. "I don't want to accuse Farah-Lajoie here, but perhaps that rope was placed on that log by the real murderer to create false evidence." He reminded the jury that the furnace stoker Leclerc had a key to the house. Germain's insinuations were clear: he wanted the jury to believe that evidence had been planted, either by the police or by Leclerc.

He next concentrated on the quilts, pointing out that they had been found in the room of one of the Delorme girls, which did not point to Adélard. Was he hoping this manoeuvre would divert attention to the sisters? He had nothing to lose and knew full well that the chances of winning an acquittal for his client increased with each doubt he could put in the minds of the jury. "Is the accused really the murderer? There were four people in the house that day, three of whom were entertaining friends. If the hope of gain can lead to crime, the disappointment in receiving nothing can also lead to the same end."

Germain, who had promised not to play on emotion, then did just that as he shifted into his spellbinding best, bringing tears to the eyes of most of the jury, "We who feel the enormity of humiliation insist on being condemned only if there is an enormity of proof." After one long hypnotic look at the jury, a satisfied Germain sat down, convinced that his six-hour plea had convinced the jury to acquit his client.

Calder rose from his chair and slowly walked towards the jury. "I congratulate my learned friend Germain, who has lived up to his high reputation. I don't have his warm eloquence, his all-encompassing speech, his talent to extract a verdict which contradicts evidence. Even if I did, I wouldn't use it, because the Crown is not seeking to win a case, it is simply searching for the truth."

His plea, which lasted two hours, was essentially a repetition of what he had said in 1923. He reminded the jury of Delorme's proven pattern of lying, as shown by his statements about Raoul's last will and his father's handgun and especially in the lies uncovered by the testimony of the telephone company employees. "No one, contrary to what Delorme said, had called him that night. That kind of lying by a man suspected of a crime is usually enough to justify a verdict of guilt." Calder also refused to believe the story about Raoul going out for a dinner "in some style" that night because, if he had done so, why was he dressed in his older clothes? As far as Calder was concerned, the evidence was clear that "either in the afternoon or the evening of 6 January, the two brothers found themselves alone at home. It wouldn't be the first crime of this kind. The first was committed by Cain."

When the Crown's plea ended, Judge Martineau began his address, despite the late hour. He first dealt with the rumour that the majority of the jury had already voted for an acquittal. "I don't want to honour such rumormongering with any reaction. I have the utmost confidence in your integrity." Like his predecessor Lemieux, Judge Martineau seemed convinced of the accused's guilt. Acknowledging that the proof was purely circumstantial, he said it could nevertheless be sufficient to prove the Crown's case. Taking the quilts as an example of circumstantial evidence, he added, "The Crown simply has to prove the similarity of the quilts and the fact that the accused had or could have had possession of them. In the absence of any evidence from the defence refuting the resulting presumption, you can properly conclude that the quilts came from the Delorme house." To emphasize his point he added, "Can you imagine any two persons each making a quilt so badly? I can conceive that two perfect quilts could have each been made by different experts, but if you consider the identical defects in the quilts shown as evidence, must you not conclude that they were made by the same person? And if you so conclude, you must then ask yourselves whether a stranger stole them from the house or if the murderer was either one of the Delorme girls or the accused. Circumstances are not counted but weighed. A single circumstance can be conclusive, whereas many circumstances would not. But a series of circumstances which, if taken alone would be meaningless, can as a whole lead to certainty. If you believe that the handgun in itself is sufficient evidence of the accused's guilt, if you believe that the bullets in and by themselves are also sufficient proof of guilt, if you believe that the quilts also point to the accused, the joining of these three pieces of evidence add to the strength of his guilt and make it an irresistible fact."

The judge thought Delorme had sufficient motive to kill his brother. "The accused knew about the will and about being its main beneficiary. It is rather strange that Raoul would have given almost everything to the member of his family who, in view of his position, needed it the least. You must also consider the false, I should say hypocritical, declarations made by the accused, his statements to Detective Pigeon denying that he knew the contents of the will when he did know the contents, his evasive answers to Roby of the where-abouts of the will when he knew he had deposited it with Notary Bélanger. These facts abundantly show that the accused had a motive for committing the crime for which he is accused." He also attached great importance to the overcoat and overshoes. "When Raoul left the house that afternoon, as claimed, is it reasonable to believe that he had left without his overshoes? It was very cold, the sidewalks were slippery and is it reasonable that a man who expected to be away until three o'clock in the morning would go without his overshoes?"

He was sure the crime had been committed at the Delorme home. On this point, he simply reminded the jury about the overshoes and the cobbler's evidence. Regarding the handgun, the gunsmith's testimony, and the ballistics tests, he asked the jury, "Doesn't this prove to reasonable men, to men conscious of the oath which they took, that all of the bullets were shot from the accused's handgun?"

The evidence about the transportation of Raoul's body gave him some trouble, said Judge Martineau. He pointed to some contradictions. "If you accept Lilly's testimony, it is certain that the accused stayed home until about one o'clock in the morning. But I submit that in law, as in fact, if all the other facts, separately or cumulatively, convince you of the accused's guilt, you don't have to ask yourselves how he transported the body to Snowdon unless such a feat would have been absolutely impossible – and you can render a verdict of guilty." Commenting on the late night telephone calls, the judge explained that it would be difficult to disbelieve the testimony of the telephone company employees and strongly suggested that the accused had lied.

In closing, the judge called on the jury not to fall into the trap of feeling pity for the accused. "It is normal to call on that sentiment in criminal cases and the learned counsel for the defence used that rule very cleverly. He used an approach which reached into your hearts, indeed into all our hearts. None of us could keep back our tears.

However, if you think the prisoner is guilty, if you think he committed this awful crime of which he is accused, a crime for which we can't find a comparable example in history, the sentiment of pity as the reason for his acquittal would be more than weakness, cowardice, and treason. It would make you his accomplices."

It was now past midnight. There was nothing else left but to adjourn and send the jury off to deliberate. It had almost been told outright to come back with a conviction.

At exactly ten o'clock next morning, 19 March, Judge Martineau entered the courtroom. Adélard Delorme followed a few moments later, looking pale and nervous. "Has the jury reached a verdict?" asked the clerk in a loud voice. Jury foreman Raoul Thibeault rose, "We cannot possibly reach agreement, your Lordship."

That didn't come as a great surprise to the judge. He addressed the jury, "The foreman has just told the Court that you cannot reach agreement, that you cannot come to a verdict. Am I to understand that it is absolutely useless to keep you any longer? Do you think that by discussing the matter further you could arrive at an agreement?" In perfect tandem each member of the jury replied, "No, we will never be able to agree." Judge Martineau did not insist. "The Court must record your report and release you. I am convinced that all of you tried to do your duty and I thank you for it. Gentlemen, you're free to go back to your families."

Totally discouraged, Delorme was taken back to Bordeaux Prison. Reporters rushed to the jurymen to discuss the verdict and learned that the division was ten to two for acquittal, an exact reversal of the preceding year's vote. However, *Le Canada* reported that a juror had told one of its reporters that until the evidence on ballistics, there had been a three way split among the jurors: nine were for acquittal, two for conviction, and one undecided. After that evidence one of the two, evidently not impressed with the science of ballistics, joined the nine. The indecisive juror moved to the acquittal side after the handwriting evidence, which he evidently didn't find sufficient, making it eleven to one. Apparently one of the eleven shifted to the conviction side after hearing Judge Martineau's plea. "Jury Does Not Agree" headlined the late edition of The *Montreal Daily Star*. The story went on to state:

Customarily a person accused of murder has been liberated by the government after three trials, though in some instances release has come after two trials. In this case it is understood that the government will send Delorme before a jury for the third time. In the event of a third disagreement, it is taken for granted that the Abbé would be released.

"What will be the fate of the accused?" screamed headlines in *La Presse's* evening edition. Calder issued a press release stating that hung juries were not a rare occurrence and that in such cases another trial was required. He added, however, that the attorney general had the power to issue a *nulli prosequi*, which would halt any further proceedings. When asked if he would withdraw from the case, he answered, "Not at all; I started the Delorme case and, God willing, I will finish it." From Quebec City, the attorney general made the following statement: "A second hung jury does not necessarily end a case. In any event, I am not ready to decide what I will do. I will wait for the crown prosecutor's report."

The decision was taken a few days later. Delorme would be tried again.

The Verdict

The fourth trial started on Monday, 13 October 1924, presided over by the Honourable Auguste Maurice Tessier. There were no changes at the lawyers' bar. Delorme had stayed with Alban Germain and Robert Calder continued for the Crown. The other familiar face was Gustave Monette, who once again was the first to rise with his ever present request for a hearing on insanity. Once again, it was denied.

Germain demanded a totally French-speaking jury. His request was granted. As a result the available jury panel, which included many English-speaking Montrealers, was disqualified and Tessier adjourned until two o'clock to allow the sheriff time to make up another panel. To do this, he immediately mobilized fifty taxicabs and dozens of policemen in the Champ-de-Mars behind the Court House and deployed them throughout the city with instructions to return with the required number of men. The scene looked like a military operation as the cabs took off in different directions, accompanied by an array of policemen and deputy sheriffs. The sheriff was authorized to use whatever force was necessary to bring his candidates to court. By two o'clock, a panel of 150 jurymen had been formed. It would not be enough. The notoriety of l'affaire Delorme had made it almost impossible to find someone who hadn't already formed an opinion on the case. Among those who hadn't, some were against capital punishment, while many declared that they would be unable to condemn a priest. The same procedure to gather candidates had to be repeated the next day, with the sheriff's motorcade combing the streets of Montreal gathering pedestrians. In all, more than 300 candidates were brought in. By the second evening, the jury had finally been formed.*

* The jury was composed of Ferdinand Ethier, Ozas Martineau, Honoré Bail, J.S. Ménard, Léo Brunet, Rosario Deslauriers, Joseph Champagne, Raphael Ménard, Cléophas Grignon, Waldy Lavallée, Alcide Riopel, and Eliodore Manse.

Interest in the case had waned. In the fall of 1924 headlines were about the impending execution of the six killers involved in the famous Hochelaga Bank murder. Judge Tessier even had to adjourn the Delorme trial for a couple of days to allow Germain and Calder, who were each representing one of the condemned, time to go to Ottawa and make representations to the federal minister of justice for a stay of execution.*

There were only a dozen or so spectators on hand when the trial resumed. By now everyone knew the script and each player filled his or her role perfectly. Both sides sprinted through the testimony. In some cases depositions from the earlier trials were simply produced in the record instead of calling the witnesses. The expert testimony on handwriting that had taken up so much time at the previous trials was eliminated altogether. Farah-Lajoie was the only one who added something. Still convinced of Delorme's guilt, he told the jury he could explain the mysterious telephone calls the night of the murder. During a recent visit to the Delorme house, he had discovered that by placing a piece of metal on one of the exposed telephone wires in Delorme's study it was possible to make the phone ring. Throughout Farah-Lajoie's testimony Delorme stared at him defiantly. Again Germain did his best to discredit the detective's testimony. "Did you not recently say to one of your colleagues, 'Finally I have gotten hold of a cassock and I won't let this one get away.'" Farah-Lajoie firmly replied, "I have too much respect for the cassock to have said such a thing."

The most significant decision during the trial was Judge Tessier's ruling that evidence from Delorme's deposition at the coroner's inquest and his statements to the police were not admissible. Not only did this reverse Judge Martineau's decision in the previous trial but Germain didn't even have to object – when the Crown tried to introduce the deposition, Tessier flatly refused it. And when Crown lawyers called the first of several detectives to testify about Delorme's statements, Tessier ordered him back to his seat.

By 30 October, the evidence was complete and the lawyers made their closing remarks. "This is the fourth time," said Germain, "that the accused has appeared before his peers to be judged on the most terrible of crimes that can weigh on a man's conscience – the crime

---

* In another sensational trial, Louis Morel (an ex-policeman), Frank Gambino, Giuseppe Sefarini, Tony Frank, Mike Valentino, and Leo Davis had been convicted of robbing the Hochelaga Bank armoured car and murdering its driver. All were condemned to hang, although at the last minute Davis and Valentino's sentences were commuted to life imprisonment. The others were executed at Bordeaux Prison in a quadruple hanging in the early dawn of 24 October 1924. Both scaffolds were used and they were hanged in pairs, back to back.

of murder. And this particular murder is alleged to have been a fratricide, whose horror is further increased because the murderer is alleged to be a priest." He ended his five and one-half hour address by asking the jury to acquit his client, to "close the file on this *cause célèbre* and throw the cloak of oblivion on one of the most horrible crimes to ever have been tried by our courts."

Calder began his address the next morning to a packed courtroom. Speaking for two and half hours he told the jury that the murder had been committed at 190 St Hubert and that if, as Florence had testified, Raoul went out in the afternoon, then he came back either later in the afternoon or during the evening. "When Raoul's body was found, he wasn't wearing his good clothes. Now Raoul was wealthy. When he went to the theatre he chose the best seats. We were told he had gone to the theatre and was later going to a stylish party. Yet he was found with his old clothes on and had left his new blue suit at home. I find that inconceivable. And if he was wearing his coat when he was shot, how can you explain the bullet hole in his jacket but none in his coat?" He told the jury that Delorme's condemnation would not reflect on the priesthood. "His shame will be his very own and his crime will have been his very own." Surprisingly, Calder finished his statement by saying that Delorme would be freed if the jury couldn't agree on a verdict. "A *nulli prosequi* or order not to proceed will be issued and Delorme will be freed."

The judge's remarks were very brief, lasting no more than half an hour and favouring a conviction. "The quilts," he said, "point to the murder having been committed at 190 St Hubert. Who would profit by the murder?" he asked. "The insurance policy, Raoul's will, the fact that Raoul would soon be taking over management of his own affairs give us the motive." Commenting on Lajoie he added, "An attempt was made to discredit the policemen in this case, particularly detective Lajoie. I refused to allow a certain line of questioning because it was illegal. However I do not see anything in Lajoie's testimony which allows us to say that Lajoie was overzealous in his duty. He did his duty. Where would we be if we had to discredit policemen because they do their duty very well?"

Like his predecessors, he felt he had to end his remarks with observations about the accused's priesthood. "To say that the accused is a priest is to insinuate that men are not equal before the law. The day on which the weak and the strong, the rich and the poor, are not equal before the law will be the day of social revolution. When a man is guilty, he must be condemned, whether he is poor, rich, weak, strong, a priest, a judge, a financier, or a beggar. You would all be frauds, gentlemen of the jury, if you took into account the social character or the standing of the accused. We have a duty to accomplish, a very painful duty. I have done my part to the end – I can only hope that you will do the same."

By one o'clock Tessier sent the jury off to deliberate, asking they return by five o'clock. "Why don't we come back earlier than that?" asked a juror. "We want to go home to our families. Tomorrow is All Saint's Day and we want too prepare for the holiday." The judge cut off an hour, saying they could return at four. But when pressed by another juror to shorten it to three o'clock, he lost patience. "This case is too important, Gentlemen. This is not a question of days or hours, but of weeks and of years. I am ready to sit for another three weeks if need be, because the life of a man is at stake. Gentlemen, the Court orders you to return at five o'clock and no sooner."

As the jury shuffled off, Delorme looked confident and gave his sisters a big smile before disappearing into the waiting cell behind the prisoner's dock. By this time the scene was reminiscent of the earlier trials. Crowds were pushing and shoving around the entrance of the courtroom trying to get a glimpse at what was going on inside. They had overflowed into the streets bringing traffic to a halt.

At five o'clock the jury returned. The clerk asked the usual: "Gentlemen of the jury, are you agreed upon your verdict?" Almost immediately the twelve jurymen answered loudly, "Not guilty." The audience reacted with a mixture of cheers and jeers but was quickly brought to order by the judge. Germain asked that his client be released from custody immediately. After a quick glance at Calder who, visibly disappointed, stated, "There is nothing further against this man, your Lordship," the judge ordered, "Let the prisoner be freed."

Elated, Delorme shook hands with his guards and Prison Governor Napoléon Séguin who, over the years, had become a friend and confident. He thanked his lawyers and, after having given Farah-Lajoie an arrogant stare, made his way to the prisoner's antechamber where he was warmly greeted by his sisters and friends. He then slipped away through a side door where a large Packard limousine was waiting with Germain inside. To the sound of cheers from a crowd of his supporters, many of whom were waving pennants, Delorme got in the car which sped off to the archbishop's palace, followed by a car full of newspaper reporters. He was greeted with open arms by Msgr Deschamps. The next morning he satisfied a wish he had expressed during his incarceration: he said his first Mass in close to three years at the Notre Dame de Lourdes chapel of St Jacques Church, where he had been ordained some fifteen years earlier.

The press reported that Delorme intended to take a long rest at the Trappist Monastery in Oka and would then apply to have the civil interdiction lifted and to collect the $25,000 insurance on Raoul's life. It was also reported that the jury had decided for acquittal within minutes after the end of the judge's remarks and that many had spent the rest of the afternoon sleeping. Jury members said that until Farah-Lajoie's testimony they had been divided on the question of Delorme's guilt. The defence's attack on the detective's credibility was the turning point. The coup de grâce was the judge's refusal to admit into testimony Delorme's deposition at the coroner's inquest and his statements to the police.

Thus ended Delorme's 989 days of custody and a series of trials that had involved a dozen judges, twenty lawyers, hundreds of witnesses, and the whole population of Montreal.*

The Delorme file was permanently closed.

---

* The judges involved in the case at both the civil and criminal levels were Victor Cusson, Dominique Monet, Arthur Bruneau, Louis Coderre, Sir François Lemieux, C.A. Wilson, Paul Gédéon Martineau, Auguste Maurice Tessier, C.E. Dorion, John Edward Martin, Blaise Letellier, and Wilfrid Mercier.

Who Killed Raoul?

I am sure Adélard Delorme murdered his brother. The Crown could not produce any eyewitnesses, but its circumstantial evidence was overwhelming. The Bayard handgun and bullets bought a few days before the murder; the ballistics tests that matched the bullets found in Raoul's head with the bullet fired from the accused's Bayard; the matching quilts, soap, and blood in the car; the expert testimony about Delorme's handwriting on the package; the testimony that his neighbours had heard his car running on the night of the murder; the tire marks leading into his garage; the unused overshoes – all pointed to him.

The motive was also clear – greed. As executor of his father's estate and manager of Raoul's affairs, Father Delorme controlled a great many assets, assets which he and Rosa would probably have inherited had their father not remarried and fathered Raoul. His lifestyle was expensive. He was a car enthusiast, liked to travel, and, from all accounts, enjoyed the company of women. He lived far beyond his means and had to use his brother's bank account to meet his debts. Two weeks before Raoul's death, he had insured his life for $25,000. Less than a year earlier, he had assisted Raoul in preparing his will, whose provisions he had probably influenced – a will that made him and Rosa the chief beneficiaries.

The most likely scenario is that Delorme had decided to murder Raoul long before the night of 6 January. He and Rosa may well have plotted the murder a year or so earlier after Adélard had helped Raoul draft his will. Delorme knew the 1921 Christmas break would be his last opportunity to commit the murder before Raoul took over management of his assets in the spring and discovered that his brother was embezzling from him. Delorme replaced his old gun with a new, quieter Bayard. Then he waited for the right moment.

Raoul's holidays, however, were ending and somehow the two of them had never been alone long enough for Adélard to carry out his plan. As the deadline grew closer, Rosa arranged to take Lilly to the theatre on the night of the sixth. Florence went to a movie with her boyfriend. I think the priest already knew that Raoul would be back around nine o'clock. That explains his nervous confusion when he answered Tassé's first telephone call by mistakingly telling him Florence was out. He also uncharacteristically declined an invitation from the Vincents to spend the evening with them. Why would he do that, being the social butterfly that he was and knowing the rest of the family would be out? Raoul did telephone around seven o'clock to tell the priest he wouldn't be home for dinner, but I think he said that he was going to a movie and would be back around nine o'clock, not that he would be having an elaborate dinner with friends and might spend the night away from home, as the priest told his half-sisters. Raoul had only stayed out overnight once before in his life and it seems odd that, being the quiet young man he was, he would have chosen the eve of his return to Ottawa to go carousing with newly made friends. Also, the report of an elaborate dinner was not supported by the slight amount of food found in his body. The only person to speak to him on the telephone that evening was Adélard. Florence and Lilly would certainly have believed whatever he told them.

After everyone had left the house, the priest had only to wait for Raoul. Shortly before nine, Raoul walked in, took off his overshoes, and headed up to his study, where he turned on some music. Then, either one of two things happened. As Raoul was listening to his record player, Delorme, wearing his duster, approached him from behind, held an ether-soaked rag against his nose, and shot him in the head. A struggle followed and when it ended, five more bullets had found their mark. Adélard then wrapped Raoul's head in the quilts to absorb the bleeding, laid his body on his bedsheets, dragged it down to the garage, and put it in the car. The second possibility is that Adélard invited Raoul to go out for a drive and murdered him in the garage, then stuffing his body into the car. The neighbours didn't hear anything because, according to their testimony, none of them was home before 10:30 that evening.

Delorme might have involved Leclerc, the furnace stoker, in disposing of the body. It's possible that Leclerc had just finished his nine o'clock furnace check and was on his way out when he either met the priest in the process of dragging the body to the garage or heard the commotion in the garage. Delorme could have immediately turned this unexpected witness into an accomplice by telling Leclerc that he would denounce him as a murderer unless he helped dispose of the body. After all, Leclerc had a key to the house and was aware of the Delorme wealth, which made him a good suspect. And who would believe the word of an illiterate stoker against that of a priest? After leaving the body in the car, they could have returned to the house, quickly straightened out Raoul's study, collected the bullets lying on the floor, dumped them in the furnace, and driven off. First, they headed for the harbour, a few blocks away, planning to dump the body into the St Lawrence River. Barry disturbed them in their attempt, so they drove on to Snowdon, via either Décarie Boulevard or Côte des Neiges Road. Reaching Snowdon junction, they dumped the body near Coolbrook Avenue and drove back to 190 St Hubert via Côte Saint Michel, where Delorme threw Raoul's cap out of the car to create a false lead. They then separated shortly before arriving at the Delorme house.

The close bond between Adélard and his natural sister, Rosa, and her preferred treatment in Raoul's will suggest that she may also have been involved. Perhaps it was no coincidence that on the day before the murder, knowing that Florence would be out on the evening of the sixth, she had invited Lilly to come to the theatre with Davis and her, leaving Adélard alone in the house. The original plan, changed by Leclerc's unforseen appearance on the scene, may have been that on her return from the theatre she would help the priest dispose of the body. In any event Adélard may have waited for her return to tell her the deed was done, which would explain the neighbour's testimony that Adélard had driven out of his garage around 11:30 that night. When he got back home, he and Rosa tried to remove the bloodstains from the car with soap and water, cleaned and oiled the Bayard, and got rid of their cleaning rags and other evidence by throwing every-thing in the furnace and actively shaking the coals to speed up the burning process. This explains the late-night activities in the furnace room. It might also explain why Lilly broke into tears during her testimony when she said she had gone down to the basement to see Delorme that night – she may also have seen Rosa helping her brother dispose of the evidence. This wouldn't have been a problem for the priest, as his Svengali-like influence on his two dull-witted half sisters would have assured him of their cooperation.

Early the next morning Delorme drove his Franklin to the garage to replace and repair the snowchains he had damaged on his late-

night race around the city's crusty streets accompanied by either Rosa
or Leclerc. He returned home just in time to greet Detectives Pigeon
and Desgroseillers, who were calling on the Delorme family to tell
them of Raoul's death. If Leclerc was involved, the priest may well
have told him to leave Montreal that afternoon.

Delorme then began fabricating evidence and playing his game of
charades with the police investigation. He made a point of keeping
in close contact with the investigation, which allowed him to take
protective measures (such as hiding his racoon coat at a nearby
convent shortly before his arrest), create false leads as the case developed, and cast doubts on Farah-Lajoie's credibility. His complete
authority over his sisters, both intellectually and materially, permitted
him to control what they said throughout the investigation and trial.
They closed ranks around him and didn't stray from the story he had
cleverly woven.

Did the Crown prosecute less forcefully because the accused was a
priest? I don't think so. There certainly appeared to be an element
of reluctance at the investigation stage, and to some extent that
continued during the insanity hearing. But by the time Calder took
over the prosecution I believe the Crown was making the best possible
effort. Yet I'm still bothered by several things. Why didn't the Crown
make more out of the two cans of ether found in Adélard's cupboard
and his knowledge that six shots had been fired into Raoul's head
before this was generally known? Considering the priest's lifestyle and
his apparent taste for wild parties, it is quite likely that he participated
in "ether frolics." But by the 1920s ether was a well-known anesthetic
and could have fit very nicely into his murder plans. As to the number
of bullets, the evidence clearly showed that until March of 1922
Doctors Derome and MacTaggart were the only two people who
knew that six bullets had been fired into Raoul's head. Yet Farah-
Lajoie testified that the accused told him about the six bullets on
9 January 1922. How could he have known that unless he had fired
them himself? In their summing up to the jury both Taschereau and
Cahan tried to diminish the impact of that evidence by saying that
the information had already been disclosed in the *Montreal Daily Star*.
The 9 January edition of that newspaper had indeed carried the story
of the murder under the heading "Six Shots through Head of
Delorme." *La Presse's* edition of the same date carried the heading
"Killers Furiously Attacked Young Raoul Delorme and Fired Eight
Bullets into His Face." However, since both stories also reported on

the coroner's inquest held that same morning, it is highly unlikely they would have appeared before the afternoon edition, which hit the streets after the time Delorme mentioned the six bullets to Lajoie. Yet Calder does not appear to have made that point in his address to the jury.

What if this trial had taken place in 1995? In my view Adélard Delorme would have been convicted.

- His cassock would have given him very little, if any protection, today. The clergy no longer has the hold on Quebec society that it enjoyed in the 1920s.
- Circumstantial evidence is now generally considered to be far more reliable than in the 1920s. The key is the development of forensics as a science. Today, circumstantial and forensic evidence is often thought to be more credible than that of eyewitnesses. This is almost a complete turnaround. At the beginning of the century, an eyewitness or a confession were almost always necessary to secure the conviction of someone accused of a major crime.
- In the 1920s the penalty for murder in Canada was hanging. Capital punishment does not exist in Canada anymore. That might also have been a factor in the acquittal.

A word about the media. L'affaire Delorme was the media trial of its day. Canadian law restricts the news media to reporting only what happens in the jury's presence. Television cameras are not permitted in the courtroom. In a trial of interest to the media, what we might see on our eleven o'clock news is a very brief factual report of the day's proceedings, sometimes illustrated by a sketch or two. Talk shows don't get involved and we don't have "colour commentators." The Rules of Practice of the Superior Court of the Province of Quebec, Criminal Division stipulate that:

Anything that interferes with the decorum and good order of the court is forbidden ...

The reading of newspapers, the practice of photography, cinematography, broadcasting or television are equally prohibited during the sittings of the Court ...

Sound recording of the proceedings and of the decision, as the case may be, by the media, shall be permitted unless the judge decides otherwise. Such recordings shall not be broadcast ...

To a large extent, that explains why juries are rarely sequestered in Canada. They can read or listen to news reports of the trial and can discuss the case with one another but with no one else – not even their families. Given that framework, if Delorme were being tried in Montreal today, the media would have found it difficult to convert due process into a media circus.

Epilogue

Little is known of what happened to Delorme after his acquittal. He didn't move back to 190 St Hubert. Instead, on orders from the Archdiocese, he moved into the Institute for the Deaf and Dumb at the corner of St Lawrence Boulevard and Jean-Talon Street. He arrived under the pseudonym of Lemay, the only name by which he was known within the institute's walls. His routine was to start each day by saying Mass, then head to an office he had rented downtown, returning in the evening. The entries for January 1925 in the records of the institute read:

January 19: The Reverend Lemay-Delorme has been sent to us for a few weeks. We have billeted him in Brother Allen's room, number 4. He has come today to make his arrangements with Brother Director and will return Monday evening.

January 20: Reverend father arrived tonight and took possession of his room.

January 21: Reverend father said Mass at 5:30, gave us his blessing, and then had breakfast. He spent the rest of his days in town managing his affairs. Today, he had dinner with the Community and is known as Lemay.

What was expected to be a stay of a few weeks became permanent residence at the institute.

His name surfaced in the news a few years later when the court allowed him to take over control of Raoul's and his father's estate. It also ordered La Sauvegarde Company to pay him the proceeds of the insurance policy on Raoul's life. Rumours continued that the Delorme properties were rented out as bordellos, and it was suggested that the units adjoining 190 St Hubert were set up in such a way that a sliding wall could convert the bordello's main parlour into the priest's study. Whenever the police raided, the sliding wall would be activated and the priest would answer the door to an embarrassed group of apologetic lawmen. Delorme appeared to be always on the periphery of other illegal activities as well and was said to have been a material witness in several narcotics trials. He lived very comfortably and his eccentricities continued. He would do anything to attract a crowd and was sometimes seen going through the motions of blessing bread wagons. Despite all this, he was never defrocked. Perhaps the Church wanted to avoid another controversy. Every year, on 1 January, he telephoned Alban Germain and Lucien Gendron, his lawyers, to wish them a healthy and prosperous year.

Rosa is said to have married a man named Alfred Shepherd and moved to Duhamel, in the lower Laurentians, where she invested in large parcels of undeveloped land. She was apparently a crack rifle shot and had a shrewd business head. Widowed in 1931, in 1937 she married Pierre Avila Cléroux and continued to buy land. She made a number of purchases shortly after Delorme's death, suggesting that she had inherited money from him. It was commonly believed in the Duhamel area that she had been in on the notorious murder. She was later institutionalized as insane and died in 1953. Florence married and dropped out of sight. Lilly died in late 1939.

As for Farah-Lajoie, l'affaire Delorme changed his life. Shortly after the publication of his book, *Ma version de l'affaire Delorme*, he was demoted from detective to advisor. The case apparently led to the breakup of his marriage and, according to his daughter Ghislaine, to his excommunication by Church authorities – although there is no evidence of this in Church records.* In 1927 he was dismissed by the Montreal Police Force. Although the reasons for his dismissal are rather vague, by then he had become a favourite of the press and his high profile media image disturbed many of his superiors. Also, public statements he had made when asked to run for alderman in Montreal's Sainte-Marie ward to the effect that the police force had to be cleaned up didn't help. He had to fight for many years before he was awarded his pension. From time to time he worked as a private detective, which was also a source of problems. In 1934 he was found guilty of fabrication of evidence in an arson case and sentenced to eight months in prison. He appealed and, acting on his own behalf, had the decision reversed. By this time his financial resources had been depleted, but

---

* Not all types of excommunications are recorded. Automatic excommunications (*excommunicatio late sententiae*) do not necessarily appear in Church records.